MW00659188

BUSINESS BASICS BOOTCAMP

THE ULTIMATE CRASH COURSE

By Mitche Graf

DEDICATION

This book is dedicated to my three incredible children- Jaycee (my baby girl), Colton (C-Train) and Sierra (my baby angel). Your Dad loves you more than my words could ever convey, and I can't wait to see what wonderful people you become. Most of what I do is because of you, and for you. I'm prouder of each of you than any parent has ever been in the history of the universe. So, to my biggest inspirations, I say thank you, and I love you to Mars and back times 10 plus infinity!

Dad

BUSINESS BASICS BOOTCAMP

THE ULTIMATE CRASH COURSE

Cover Design: Ryan Lause
Back Cover Photo: Tami Graf
Publisher: Power Marketing 101
P.O. Box 405
Aurora, Oregon 97002 USA

FOR BULK ORDERS OR GROUP DISCOUNTS
CALL: 888.719.4692
www.MitcheGraf.com
ISBN: 978-1-7320344-4-0

Table of Contents

About Your Captain For This Flight

Best-selling author, lifestyle entrepreneur, internationally-renowned business speaker, former All-American Track & Field athlete, and Daddy-of-Three Mitche Graf has been a passionate serial entrepreneur for over 25 years, dangling his toes into the ponds of many intriguing industries along the way.

From selling used bicycle parts out of his garage in the seventh grade to running three companies today, he has prided himself on knowing how to squeeze every drop of potential out of his endeavors.

Over the past three decades, Mitche has created two award-winning restaurants, a bustling internationally-known catering & events company, a national spice manufacturing business with over 4000 accounts, a photography studio, a cribbage board manufacturing company, an award-winning limousine business, a portable hot tub rental business, a drive-through espresso company, an educational products company, an athletic fitness testing corporation, and even a nightcrawler company.

In the middle of all this, he also was given the once-in-a-lifetime opportunity to become the President of Business Operations for an affiliate of the world champion San Francisco Giants baseball team.

Having started, built, and successfully operated numerous enterprises in a multitude of industries has taught him a simple truth: the same basic business principles apply, regardless of the arena you may play in.

As an educator and motivational speaker, Mitche's high-voltage seminars and workshops have been delivered around the world to over 75,000 people in 9 countries and nearly every state in the U.S., and his techniques have resulted in over $1,000,000,000 in sales from his innovative ideas. His cutting-edge articles and columns have appeared in the pages of business trade magazines such as Rangefinder, PPA Magazine, Limo Digest, Chauffer Driven, Image Maker, and Fresh Cup Magazine, as well as many online marketing sites and blogs.

He is passionate about the outdoors and laughing, playing guitar, reading, listening to great music, cooking and eating, drinking good wine, taking a tremendous amount of time off to chill, and most importantly, spending time with his family.

Mitche lives in a small country town in Oregon with his wife Tami and their three small children Jaycee, Colton, and Sierra, Tilly & Delilah the Dogs, Coral the Hermit Crab as well several hundred guppies (names not important).

He spends much of his time looking for ways to work smarter, not harder, so he can spend more time doing and enjoying the things in life that are most important to him.

He believes that *EVERY DAY IS A SATURDAY* with the right attitude, and this perspective inspires him to wake up every day with a sense of excitement and enthusiasm to live his life by design.

Sit back, relax, and enjoy the flight.

INTRODUCTION

Once upon a time, a very big, strong woodcutter got a job working for a local business. The pay was great and so were the benefits. The woodcutter was excited and determined to do his absolute best to impress the boss. His boss gave him an axe and showed him the area where he was to work.

On the first day, the woodcutter brought back twenty-five trees. *"That's great,"* said the boss. *"Keep up the good work!"* Totally motivated by his boss's encouragement, the woodcutter tried even harder the second day, but he could only bring back fifteen trees. On the third day, he only brought back ten trees. Day after day, he kept bringing back fewer and fewer.

"Something's wrong with me," the woodcutter surmised. *"I'm losing my strength."* He went to the boss and apologized, saying he could not understand what was going on.

"When was the last time you sharpened your axe?" asked the boss.

"Sharpened my axe? I don't have time; I've been too busy cutting down trees".

This book is about helping you keep your edge sharp. It's very easy to get caught up in the "cutting down of trees" that we forget to continue to sharpen our axe so that the business forest is easier to navigate.

I'm excited to spend some time with you, and I hope you are just as excited to immerse yourself in the business side of your business. The fact that you are investing your time in this book shows that you are one of the chosen few who will make a difference in your industry. I welcome and congratulate you!

In today's overcrowded marketplace, we have more choices than ever and are faced with more decisions than we've had in the past. How do we decide what we should spend our hard-earned money on? In 1980 there were 400 mutual funds; today there are over 20,000. Back just a couple of decades ago, 1500 new products hit the grocery stores shelves each year; this year there will be over 25,000. With all these choices, you have to offer something the buyers in your target demographic can't get from anyone else. You need a business plan that is brilliant in its simplicity.

The journey you are about to take is going to change your life forever... While that's a big statement, I guarantee that if you take the principles outlined here seriously, you will tap into a better way of looking at your business and create a better quality of life.

What is the number-one reason for starting your own business? Is it the joy of being a self-employed entrepreneur and an ability to dictate your own hours and have freedom to do what you want? Is it the money? Is it the ability to "breathe life" into your own business creation and watch as it grows and becomes more profitable and successful over time?

All these ideals prompt people to put everything on the line and start their own business. However, the number-one reason is that we have a passion for what we do.

If you are reading this book, I assume you are committed to building your business, or starting one. Regardless of the industry you have chosen, I suspect you are very good at what you do- whether it be building houses, selling insurance, selling groceries, or offering dog-walking services- but that doesn't mean you will be successful.

Building a business is hard work and will require the passion you already have for doing what you do, plus having a foundation of understanding of what it takes to give people something valuable in exchange for their money. Having this basic level of business acumen is vital to your future survival, and this book will teach you those skills.

During our time together, I'll challenge your mind, get your creative juices flowing, and turbocharge your passion in fresh, innovative ways. I'll teach you how to make your phone ring, drive traffic to your website, and construct the lifestyle of your dreams.

It's easy to fall into that old management trap and get caught up in the day-to-day business details. We end up running our business instead of designing our lives. We answer phones, order supplies, respond to e-mails and social media posts, clean the bathrooms, mow the lawn.

Before we know it, we are working seven days a week, sixteen hours a day- week after week, month after month. We don't have time for our families, to drop a fishing line in the lake, to hit that golf ball up and down the fairway, or to even sit on the back deck in solitude for a moment. The things that are most important to us start slowly slipping away, and we become a slave to our business rather than its master. Go to your window. Look outside. Look closely. What do you see?

Just ten doors from you, in every direction you look, a millionaire lives. Quietly. Without attracting too much attention. Ten doors from that millionaire, there's another one. And on and on it goes. One in ten Americans holds a net worth of over one million dollars. Each one of them fought the exact same doubts.

Yet, seemingly against all odds, they all made it. And to make things even weirder, it seems that the less they work, the more they are acquiring. Funny, isn't it? How's that even possible?

Well, contrary to widely preached demagogues, it's not the hard work that makes a millionaire. Just think of all the people you know who are working two jobs and still struggling to meet the ends.

So, if the "work-hard-until-you-drop-dead" dogma isn't the winning recipe, what is?

It's straightforward. And I'm going to reveal it to you. Step by step. Chapter by chapter. Until we build up your ability to have tunnel vision for your lifestyle and financial success.

Experienced. Practical. Unconventional. Modern. Not bound by formalities. Eager to pass my experience on to you. My goal for this book is simple…to release the creative juices that are inside of you to the point that you become a force unlike anything this world has ever seen.

How about we insert the coin and press play?

CHAPTER 1

Lifestyle Design

This book is intended to be the ultimate brainstorming session for your life.

It's about life... and business. All rolled up into one tidy package for you to consume. Before we begin, I want to ask you a simple question:

If you could find a way to only work twenty-four hours a week, seven months a year, and have the rest of the time to do the things in life that are most important to you, would you be interested? My bet is that your answer is a resounding "YES!" I call this the *NEW 24/7 Mentality* and it has been my driving beacon for most of my adult life. For most of my career, I have tried to be so efficient with what I do that I was able to work only 24 hours a week, 7 months a year, and have the rest of the time to do with what I chose. It hasn't always worked out that way, but that has been the shining beacon on the hill that kept me striving for a better tomorrow.

It's been said many times before by people much smarter and

wiser- and probably better looking than myself- that building a profitable business requires sacrificing everything in order to be counted as a successful enterprise. You will hear it from the gurus, you will read it in just about every business-type book, and you will witness it in practically every corner of the business world.

Work hard; twenty-hour days if necessary; sacrifice your personal time with family and friends; put your hobbies and interests on the shelf; be willing to give up almost everything in order to give your business the best chance for success. This book… is *NOT* about that.

Twenty years before being a "lifestyle entrepreneur" was a thing, I was living it. For most of my adult life, I have been called a rebel, a status-quo disruptor, an innovator, and a trailblazer. Likely because I was dropped on my head when I was young, but also because I tend to typically take the road less travelled in my business ventures and in life. If everyone else seems to be doing things a certain way, I'll be the guy not lined up like a lemming to follow the leader.

If the other kids were selling lemonade for .25 cents, I would be the kid selling it for .50 cents, but I would give you a free fresh-baked cookie. Always looking for the different angle.

No matter what adventure I am on, the underpinning of my motivation has always been to find ways to work less so I had more time to enjoy my life. I'm not lazy by any means; I just don't want to spend all my time working… plain and simple. So, I have spent most of my career looking for ways to work less and live more. THAT is what this book is truly about.

I am totally in love with what I do for a living, but I don't want to work anymore than I absolutely must to support the lifestyle I have built for myself. I have found that it's not necessary to spend unlimited hours immersed in my businesses to the point that I don't remember my kids' names, forget about the game, or neglect to take the car to the mechanic for a tune-up. It's not worth it!

Who Is This Book For?

This book is written with the distinctive goal of giving "meat and potatoes" insights to the following types of people:

- Entrepreneurs who feel overwhelmed because their businesses have taken over their lives. I know the pain that comes from being in a rut. However, as a serial Lifestyle Entrepreneur, I can tell you that adversity being the mother of necessity propels you to quantum leaps of self-improvement and prosperity.
- Wannabes with dreams of branching out on their own and starting businesses. This book will inspire you with behind-the-scenes glimpses of my three decades of creating, building, and running companies. Becoming an entrepreneur is truly one of the most deeply satisfying experiences you can ever have, and I would love nothing more than for you to get a fire under your butt to roll the dice and see what number comes up!
- Regular, older folks who want to increase the quality of their lives. This book contains golden nuggets that can give you a new set of eyes for what's truly important to enrich your life even more.

Whether you own a business or not, anyone with a dream of placing their lifestyle before their job or business is what I call an UNLEASHED ENTREPRENEUR (UE). Someone with the spirit and gumption to want a better life for themselves and their families.

I will share a vast plethora of cutting-edge business ideas, some counterintuitive approaches to running a successful enterprise, and a few inspirational stories. This book will illustrate important facts about living a passionate life as an entrepreneur in charge of your own destiny.

The bottom line is this: I want you to hand-craft the perfect life for yourself and your family, then work backwards and reverse-engineer your business to meet those goals. This book is a blueprint on how you can do just that.

I've put in long days, long weeks, long months, and long years building brands that failed and succeeded. If you're in business, or thinking about taking the leap, that means you're not alone, and neither am I. We can learn from each other.

I did it for a distinct reason. It was all part of my master plan to create a phenomenal life. Over the course of my journey, I built successful brands that employed wonderful people, created needed products and services for my customers, and generated tremendous profits. It's wired in my DNA, and I love the steep climb!

What Is Your CORE

There's an entrepreneurial flame deep inside my soul, and I assume you have that same flame, that never goes out. It's the voice in my head and heart urging me on, even when there is silence. This voice constantly instills in us the desire to make a profound difference in the world for the people that I call my CORE: my family, closest friends, and employees.

We all have this CORE group at the center of our universe. It's what gives us a distinctive reason to get up each day and put on our boots.

If you're a business owner, you're hopefully brimming over with the desire to become the very best you possibly can be. There is an innate desire to reach for goals that seem unreachable. Some are lying just below the surface, but some have been deeply buried for so long, it will take time to dig them out.

Maybe it's that dream you have of someday starting your own online marketing business; you put it aside because of your kids, your job, or life's emergencies. Well, guess what? The stars will never line up completely, and there is never a better time than right now to jump in with both feet!

It's human nature to have something to gravitate to all the time and to keep striving for, but in today's world, it's easy to let our goals slowly slip into oblivion and become a distant memory if we aren't careful.

If someone asked us, we would readily acknowledge that we want life to be exciting, but some of us have gotten too comfortable and content sitting on the couch. We need a challenge, but only a few of us ever dare to follow our hearts.

Impassioned people put everything on the line to start their own businesses. However, the main reason is still that we have passion for what we do. The gardener who starts a nursery, the weekend BBQer who opens a restaurant, the woodworker who starts a cabinet shop, or the teacher who opens a daycare.

We all share a common passion for what we do. There is absolutely nothing wrong with wanting to monetize your passion and turn it into an actual job or business. That is the American Dream at full strength!

In the old days, the word "entrepreneur" meant someone who owned their own business, plus other not-so-sexy innuendoes. It also meant someone who worked long hours, didn't spend enough time with his or her family, risked everything they had to accomplish their goals, and lived on the edge of insanity.

Today, a new breed of amazing folks is breaking the old molds, creating their own rules, and blazing innovative new trails to pursue and attain their dreams with gusto and determination. There is a big tidal wave that is quickly sweeping the business world and it's a philosophy that is flipping traditional business models on their heads.

These new UEs want to work less, play more, and redefine what it means to be a success.

They put their families and personal lifestyle choices first, then build their income blueprints based on these choices. This progressive trend exemplifies a reverse hierarchy of traditional business goal setting. It redefines what it means to have a successful brand.

To many traditional business owners, this type of thinking leads to doom and gloom. They wonder how a business can survive unless the ownership and management are willing to give up their souls to accomplish maximum profitability. They wonder how anyone can claim to be successful unless the business can scale to ten, one hundred, or one thousand employees and show doubling or tripling net profits year over year.

In my opinion, bigger isn't necessarily better. You will see examples of that throughout this book.

To a UE like myself, setting such outdated, outrageous goals today are secondary to attaining the satisfaction I get from spending time with my family, personal projects, and rewarding lifestyle activities.

If It's Not A "Hell Yes", Then It's A Big Fat No

In my case, if something doesn't help me to attain my ultimate lifestyle goals, I take a pass on it. I am constantly asked to sit on Boards of Directors for companies, encouraged sit in on meetings that have no relevance to my ultimate objectives, or encouraged to take on projects that will only "slow my roll" and not lead to a better life. I do my fair share of volunteering and give plenty to charities, but I do NOT want to be that guy that says yes to everything. I constantly must ask myself if the activity will help me achieve my ultimate goals.

Basically, if it's not a "HELL YES" then it must be a "BIG FAT NO!"

Your default answer to all new tasks or activities that require your attention must be "NO." End of discussion. More on this later.

When I began thinking this way, I recalibrated the way that I approached creative problem solving and found innovative, out-of-the-box solutions. Sadly, most people have no reason to think like this unless they are faced with a devastating event.

The goal of any successful UE is to find out how other businesses in your arena are operating, then don't do that! You want to run as fast as you can in the opposite direction and figure out ways to stand out in a crowded space. That is the sure-fire method of separating yourself from the rest of the pack.

I intentionally avoid replicating their structures, master marketing plans, and, most importantly, their systems. I've discovered this is one of the biggest killers of the entrepreneurial spirit because many systems are inefficient at best and self-destructive at worst. It kills many a dream.

Typically, many businesses are put together with the old-fashioned system of "business first, personal life last," which intrudes unforgivingly upon the business owners' lives.

Why would I want to bring on pain in replicating the way these things are done? Most traditional businesses run on the upside-down pyramid that says your business is at the top of the food chain, with your lifestyle towards the bottom. That just doesn't make sense to me whatsoever.

This inverse strategy keeps my mind focused on priorities I value, while also giving me a laser-focused approach to getting my work done quickly and efficiently. This is how a true UE approaches creating something new and exciting.

I'm decorated with honor badges of trial-and-error, setbacks, and victories, but I've always been a willing participant in the process.

I've lived the better part of my life with this simple yet very effective UE approach.

This book is going to show you how to attain your own levels of personal and business freedom with this perspective. It's not an easy move, but you'll *NEVER* want to go back to old-school rigmarole and stagnation when you make these changes.

Do you consider yourself as having an entrepreneurial spirit, regardless of whether you own a business? If you currently are a card-carrying member of the club, we are kindred spirits.

If not, maybe you know deep down that you are destined to become one of the chosen few.

You Might Be an Entrepreneur If…

I love Jeff Foxworthy and his "You Might Be A Redneck If" one-liners. They have become as American as apple pie and Chevrolet.

Well, you too might be an Unleashed Entrepreneur if:

- You have an insatiable desire to live a kick-ass life full of meaning and purpose
- You get bored easily and can't stand wasting time
- You have a deep motivation to overcome the odds, no matter how unlikely
- You have an unbridled optimistic feeling about the world and your life, even when others around you ooze pessimism
- You prefer to break the rules instead of living within them
- You stay away from low-energy people and their negative influences
- You have an affinity towards risk-taking, small or large
- You have ideas rattling around in your head all the time and can't wait to try them out
- You ask for forgiveness after, instead of permission before
- You passionately study how winners operate to learn their secrets

- You are constantly trying to learn new stuff
- You write your goals down on paper
- You bounce back rapidly from failures and try again
- You enjoy interacting with people smarter than you, so they inspire you
- You work hard and play even harder!

If you answered yes to at least five of the above bullet points, I'm delighted to say that you are wired to be an Unleashed Entrepreneur, meaning we are cut from the same cloth!

If you answered yes to ten or more, you are officially a VIP member with a seat in the front row of life! Congratulations!

What Kills Passion

These skills are sometimes inherently inside of you, but often must be nurtured and developed over time and must come with a dose of passion and purpose.

However, purpose and motivation don't strike us like lightning. These good habits must be cultivated through practice and patience. The exuberant enthusiasm that seeps from every cell of your body is not a feeling or a mood. You must act.

Let's discuss some common deterrents preventing us from unleashing our potential as successful UEs.

Procrastination

I believe the biggest killer of our motivation and passion is procrastination. This unfortunate malaise is caused by our misunderstanding that doing certain tasks will cause us some sort of pain.

Against that perceived pain, we must balance the enormous benefits.

Do any of these thoughts sound familiar?

- I'll get to it TOMORROW
- I'll take the kids to the park NEXT weekend. I'll make that trip to Alaska when I retire
- Maybe when I'm older
- Perhaps when I'm more settled in my job
- Maybe when the kids are out of the house
- I'll buy that big TV I've been wanting for the last two years as soon as the old one breaks down

What if that day never comes? No matter what your circumstances are in life, you will always come up with reasons why something can't be done. Instead, why not come up with one great reason why you should?

Procrastination can be the great robber of our time if we're not careful. Nothing will suck out the vigor for life faster than a good case of it. Show me a garage stuffed with "I'll get to it later" projects, and I'll show you a life that is not reaching its full potential. Nothing can stop a dream faster than our own laziness.

Well, today is the first day of the rest of your life! You can begin now to take control of your life and get back to that feeling of relevance and contentment.

Check out this piece of anonymous wisdom about procrastination:

They were going to be all that they wanted to be... tomorrow.

None would be braver or kinder than they... tomorrow.

A friend who was troubled and weary, they knew, would be glad of a lift— and needed it too.

On him they would call—see what they could do... tomorrow.

Each morning they stacked up the letters they'd write... tomorrow. The greatest of people they just might have been, the world would have opened its heart to them.

But, in fact, they passed on and faded from view, and all that they left when their living was through was a mountain of things, they intended to do... tomorrow.

I can't impress upon you enough that you must take action today. If you can't see yourself realizing the dream, you never will. Just when you're about ready to succeed, something will surely pull you back. If you feel overwhelmed, break it down and get started!

After all, you can't eat an elephant all at once, can you? Start breaking down the big things in your life into small, manageable tasks to eat one bite at a time.

Ah, but there's always tomorrow, right?

Working Hard or Smart?

How many people do you know that work two or even three jobs, yet still struggle to meet the ends? Heck, maybe you're one of those people.

Working hard is admirable alright, but in the long run it won't make you A) a fortune and B) happy. It might have worked for the older generations like the Silent Gen and Baby Boomers and even some Gen X's, but in this day and age, that paradigm became obsolete.

Today is about working smart – regardless of the invested hours. Plus, working smart means fewer doctor's appointments in a futile attempt to fix that damaged spine, hypertension or high cholesterol—all caused by overexposure to the modern day's stress and anxiety.

"Unleashed Entrepreneurs are constantly looking for ways to become more efficient, thus giving them more time to NOT work"

But what does it mean to work smart rather than hard? In a nutshell: Working smart means investing your full capacities in the most profitable segments of your operations and delegating everything else.

Things that are certain hypes these days like micromanaging and multitasking don't belong to the concept of smart work.

"An Unleashed Entrepreneur looks into the future. Everything that is present or past is someone else's job"

Take retail day traders. These guys commonly make six or seven figures a year without even blinking, let alone investing some hard labor into it. Their trick is looking into the future.

A whole army of analysts is preparing daily, weekly, monthly and Y-on-Y reports. A trader simply decides whether to go long or short. His only concern is the future. The army dwells on the past and present situation.

Or take me. Three-plus successful businesses, plus being the President of Business Operations for an affiliate of the world champion San Francisco Giants. You would think that I don't even have the time to brush my teeth, let alone shoot some hoops with my son, or watch my oldest daughter's swim meet, or go to lunch with my youngest daughter at her school, or spend time with my wife.

You just need to let go of one common, well-rooted dogma that society and your parents planted in your mind while you were just a kid.

Balancing Private and Professional

Now, if you really aren't concerned about anything outside of your business endeavors, that's completely ok. You have my permission to put this book down and return to your unending work.

On the other hand, if you are a human being that needs support from your loved ones, like I am, hear me out now, and hear me well.

By far, the most asset that you and I possess is time, and the biggest decision we have daily is how we choose to spend it.

We have 86,400 seconds each day. How we consciously choose to spend those seconds determines who we ultimately become over a lifetime.

Each day, we literally make hundreds of decisions that determine what kinds of successes or failures our businesses will endure. Many of these seconds, minutes, and hours are wasted on thoughts and activities that add zero value to our lives or the lives of the people who mean the most to us. And once that time is spent, we can never get it back.

Leaving my corporate job back in the 1994 provided a real shock to my system. The School of Hard Knocks was about to open its doors to me. If I didn't do it correctly, there would be a deep grave of failed business corpses waiting at the end of the proverbial hallway of doom.

I knew my chances of success were low. I was aware half of all businesses ended within their first year, 80% were gone within five years, and 96% failed within 10 years. I had started and built several businesses before then, but this was the first time I was going to be all in with no fallback. For those of you who have started a business at some point in your life, you know exactly what I'm talking about.

Even with doom and gloom staring at me in the face, my only thought was: *Hooray, I'm going to be one of the 4% who will make it as an entrepreneur!*

There's an excitement that wells up inside. A surreal calm that overtakes the inner fears of the prospective businessperson. In fact, the excitement can be so magnificent that it's difficult to shut off the river of creative ideas flowing at every waking moment of the day.

I knew my odds were low, but I had a big advantage over failure. I had the rare ability to live EVERY DAY LIKE A SATURDAY!

In other words, I don't get the Monday morning blues or get stuck in the rut of a nine-to-five work week mentality.

The Awakening

This life-changing philosophy was instilled in me by my stepfather, Pat Wright, one of the hardest working men I've ever met. He loved my mom deeply, and that motivated him to do whatever was necessary to keep us safe and secure.

You see, my parents divorced when I was eleven, and my mom worked two or three jobs at a time to provide for my brother, sister and me. We would see Dad on weekends, but the day-to-day raising of us kids was all Mom. Pat came into our lives several years later, and by that time we were a tribe of hardened souls accustomed to doing without in many cases, but never lacking in the important things in life.

When I was in my early 20s, Mom and Pat dreamed of owning a boat. Not a big, fancy boat to sail the seven seas in, but a boat the family could take to Hayden Lake in North Idaho where we could spend our weekends floating off into warm, summer evenings.

With this dream in mind, they managed to set aside enough money to realize their dream. They eventually found and bought Big Red, an old V-hulled Fiberform. The excitement in our family was incredibly palpable. She was an older vessel that needed a paint job and some TLC, but she had class.

We bought Pat his very first captain's hat, loaded the cooler with beer and water, and set sail.

I distinctly remember to this day how the five of us left the marina with smiles in tow on a beautiful summer day. With our troubles behind us, we fell into total silence as we looked around and gazed at the beautiful mountains and shorelines. We were without a care in the world. Nobody was going to take away the beauty of that moment from us.

The awesome silence was broken by Pat's immortal words. *"I wonder what the poor folk are doing today."*

Those words hit home. We suddenly felt elevated to a higher plane at that singular moment. We were all in Never-Never Land for that tiny little slice of our awesome day that nobody could take away from us. An amazing feeling of euphoria floated in our minds, however fleeting.

My mother responded, *"Babe, we are the poor folk."* Her words were true to the core in the practical sense; but on that day, practicality was out the window.

Pat affectionately looked at each of us, then looked out to the horizon with his chest puffed up and his head held high, and said:

"Not today, Babe, not today."

At that precise moment, we became the richest people on planet Earth—and it had nothing to do with money!

You can have all the money in the world, but if you don't have someone precious to share it with, it won't matter. And that's exactly what will happen if you let your professional life take over.

Those brief moments of joy we feel every time a child smiles from the deepest depths of his heart, or erotic arousal when our partner slowly leans on us are all we've got. Someday, not so far from now, you'll find yourself sitting in a chair, in front of a window, remembering. Those few reminiscences will be all you have left. Did you build an environment potent enough to create an emotion so powerful that it can create a long-lasting memory? A single memory that could trigger joy and excitement once again even decades after?

Whether you like it or not, one thing will always tip the scale and it's up to you to decide which one it will be.

The Disruptive 24/7 Paradigm

Unleashed Entrepreneurs work diligently to reinvent the ways in which they put their life together, and how they approach what they do for a living. In living a balanced life, they want to:

- Work smarter so they can spend more time doing OTHER THINGS!
- Work less so they can spend more time doing OTHER THINGS!
- Reinvent how they run their businesses so they can spend more time doing OTHER THINGS!

To sum up, they basically wanted to work less and live more!

I've always approached my life like a bull in a china shop. But one thing I can say about my philosophy of *"Making Every Day a Saturday"* is that you only live this life once, so you'd better make it count!

The zeal for living that I've always possessed deep in my gut has fueled me for as long as I can remember. I became determined not to become a prisoner to my businesses, but to live life like I really meant it! Now it's time for you to pull the same prank on the system and established paradigms.

As I mentioned earlier, I have a "24/7 Mentality," but not in the way you have believed your entire life. When you hear "24/7," what do you immediately think of?

Most people think of twenty-four hours a day, seven days a week. This typically refers to someone who keeps his or her nose to the grindstone all the time, or a business that never closes, right?

Does this sound like anyone you know? I believe this describes a very large population in the world these days. However, my definition of the 24/7-work mentality is quite different.

To me, it means twenty-four hours a week, seven months a year. Let that soak in a minute.

EXERCISE: Building Your "Perfect Day"

A potter knows that to end up with something worthwhile, they must know ahead of time what they are making. If you simply threw the lump of clay onto the potter's wheel without knowing what you wanted to make, you'd end up with the same lump. You must have an idea of what you're trying to accomplish—before you begin the process of formation and transformation.

Likewise, the caterpillar's calling to become a butterfly means it must strain, grow, stretch, and change within the confines of its chrysalis. Before it emerges from its sheltered cocoon to fly away, the caterpillar must struggle and strain to get out of its prison and fulfill its destiny. It's a process to grow and mature. Just like the caterpillar, you're not meant to stay inside a cocoon forever. You're meant to fly!

With that said, the process of imagining "a perfect lifestyle" can give us leeway to craft "a perfect day."

To be able to work twenty-four hours a week, seven months a year, and use the rest of your time to do whatever is important to you, you'll have to radically change the way you approach your business. You'll need to deconstruct your pre-conceived notions of what success means on the deepest levels. Would you be a willing participant in this process if you knew there was a pot of gold waiting for you at the end of the virtual rainbow? Sure, you would.

Start with The End, And End with The Beginning.

Let me tell you what a perfect day is for me. I would wake up at 4:00 AM, feeling refreshed both physically and emotionally. After spending time outside with our dogs, Tilly & Delilah, I'd enjoy a fresh-brewed cup of good coffee with half-and-half and honey.

The table next to my recliner would be piled high with books and magazines that I'd be ecstatic to dive into. I'd have some new-age jazz, classic rock, or a podcast playing away in my headphones. Once I checked my sports scores, the news, and weather for the day, I'd spend the first two hours immersed in self-improvement activities to get my juices flowing. All private time with no interruptions.

The next hour would be spent in the REFLEX ZONE responding to the world's requests for my time. I'd reply to emails, honey-do lists, and other activities centered on the demands on my time from outside sources.

After that, I'd wake my kids from their night's slumber and help them get ready for their day. With kids ranging from ages five to fourteen as I write this book, each has their own unique morning rituals and personality traits. On my perfect day, they would have different start times for school, allowing me the chance to converse with them individually. Daddy bonding time would be a precious way of getting to know them just a little bit better before the day began for us.

I would send each off to school with the biggest hug in the world, and an amazing affirmation of, "I LOVE YOU TO MARS AND BACK TIMES INFINITY PLUS TEN!" They would know beyond a doubt their Daddy loves them more than any other Daddy has ever loved their kids.

My wife Tami and I would have a tremendously engaging and productive morning meeting, talking about everything from our kids and family plans to the agenda for our workday. Just a nice slice of time with my wife talking about life!

Then, it would be time to go to work. During my pre-planned work hours, I'd be uber-efficient with my responsibilities, such as making calls, writing projects, team meetings and training, product evaluations, recording podcasts, and other business activities.

All these activities would be put into a "POD." In my definition, it means a section of time dedicated to a singular task or series of similar tasks without the influence of outside forces. We will talk more about the POD system a bit later.

I want to have the best time anyone can legally have while working. Remember, I love what I do so much that I believe I haven't worked a single day since the spring of 1994, so it's very easy for me to imagine this. Short, sweet, and to the point. I would get maximum results for minimal amounts of effort expended. Work time done, back to the fun!

There'd be a fishing pole and a pack of night crawlers waiting for me as soon as I was done working, I'd spend an hour catching the biggest trout you ever saw! The fish would put up a great fight before finally being defeated by my outstanding fishing skills. On the way home, I'd have inspiring phone conversations with my Mom, and my Dad.

By the time I got home, the kids would be getting off the school bus. I'd proceed to hear about their day's activities and help them with homework.

We would then adjourn to the kitchen to prepare a delicious five-course meal, each member of the family preparing a course that would fit in with our chosen culinary theme.

After dinner, a family board game or some guitar playing, playing with our dogs Tilly & Delilah, listening to my fourteen-year-old play her flute, watch my twelve-year-old son's hermit crab, or play dungeon with my five-year-old daughter. Laughing until my sides hurt, then more laughing.

After shower and reading time, it would be bedtime for all the munchkins while reviewing our day together. I would try to squeeze just a few more minutes and moments of happiness out of them.

Then, I'd head downstairs to finish up with any incomplete projects for the day, spend time with Tami, and cap it all off with a relaxing sauna and a hot shower. Lastly, I'd read in bed until I slowly drifted off into slumber for the night.

What a perfect day that would be! All my favorite people and experiences rolled up into a single day.

Does it sound too simple? Maybe. Then again, I can tell you that it happens on a regular basis in my life. I have a perfect day ALL THE TIME!

I call these type of perfect days **"LEVEL I"** days. It's a day I love replicating repeatedly, and they have become the cornerstone of my own perfect lifestyle. Such days are filled with the people and things I love, and outcomes I can anticipate. Do these days have setbacks and surprises? Absolutely. But I try to be flexible and roll with the adversity and unexpected surprises.

If I keep the big picture in mind, the perfect day seems to work itself out, even with occasional bumps along the road. My bar is set at a level where I know I can be successful consistently, instead of setting myself up for failure.

All too often, people set the bar so high that it would take a few miracles to achieve success at any level. It makes much better sense to reward yourself with mini victories along the way, doesn't it?

I have other types of perfect days as well.

LEVEL II includes achievable goals, events, and experiences that can't be replicated every day, such as:

- Watching a championship game with any of my teams playing: the LA Dodgers, Angels, Lakers, USC Trojans, UCLA Bruins, LA Kings, Colorado State Rams, Gonzaga Bulldogs, the Arkansas Razorbacks, or John Daly the golfer. Unfortunately, many of my teams don't make it to their respective championship games, but I'm a true fan. I hurt for days, even weeks when we lose a tough game. But I keep the dream alive 365 days a year! Sports fans, you know exactly what I'm talking about. Win or lose, we're their biggest fans!

- Attending a concert for one of my favorite artists
- Spending a holiday celebration with my immediate family
- Launching a new product or service for one of my companies
- Giving a seminar to a large group of hungry entrepreneurs and hearing about their successes
- Spend the entire day in a workshop networking with other likeminded UEs
- Hitting annual sales projections
- Taking the motorhome on a mini vacation to the mountains and finding a secluded spot

LEVEL III perfect days are goals, events, and experiences that require extensive planning, discipline and commitment, such as:

- Hanging out on the beach in Mexico for a month without a single thing to do except eat and scuba dive
- Taking a month off with the motorhome and living in the mountains, waking up every morning to the sound of a rushing river and singing birds
- Buying or selling a business
- Being with my kids when they reach lifetime milestone markers, such as their first steps, first day out of diapers, first straight-A report card, first time driving, graduation, weddings, and the birth of every grandchild.

I could go on for an entire chapter listing the different types of perfect days, but I think you get the point.

These are individual, single events happening in life, but I have created the vision in my mind of how a perfect day can be built around these activities. I want to have perfect days all the time! I work hard to keep that vision strongly embedded in my brain.

I want my life to be filled with the best days ever, one right after the next. I don't mind meeting and overcoming setbacks that stand in the way because I know the best things in life require a little pain on occasion.

You may look at my day as a simpleton at work, and I thank you for the compliment! I am passionate about the pursuit of happiness in my life; this has become the cornerstone of what a perfect day means to me. I suggest you seriously consider this core idea for your emotional health and the health of your business.

We each have a different ideal lifestyle, and that is great. Your day is unique to you and nobody else in the universe.

I truly believe I can have perfect days. I also truly believe you can experience them as well.

Does this sound counter-intuitive to the way you're used to setting goals or taking on challenges? To truly live the unleashed life, this step is a vital piece to the puzzle, as you'll discover.

Our lives are made up of dreams, goals, aspirations, wants, desires, and unmitigated passions. Many of us may talk a good game, but we tend to fumble the ball on the five-yard line when it comes to the follow-through.

Don't feel bad if this sounds like you. The world is full of people who have a difficult time finishing what they start. It's very easy to get sidetracked or lose focus on the goals we have set, especially with endless forces vying for our time and attention. The sad part is we have allowed our time to be hijacked right in front of our very eyes.

Success is achieved with a series of mini steps that will

ultimately take you to the finish line. You're basically planning and working backwards with your entire life, which will then give you the vision of what needs to get done.

Let's say that tomorrow you can have the best day of your life. No rules, no limitations. When you go to bed tonight, you know tomorrow will be your ideal day. Would that change your perspective on how you approached the day?

Crafting Your Perfect Day

Before we begin, when was the last time you remember having a perfect day? How many perfect days have you had over this past week, month, or year? How do they make you feel? Are you having a tough time coming up with answers quickly?

As we create your "Holy Grail Day," you'll need to consciously try not to let emotions and routines get in your way of building your new house. We're bulldozing your current lifestyle all the way down to the foundation, throwing out your preconceived notions of what total contentment means to you, and rebuilding a much better frame.

To begin, ask the following questions, reflect on your answers, and write them all down.

- What would your perfect day look like to you?
- What activities would you do?
- Where would you go?
- Who would accompany you?
- What kinds of food would you eat?
- What music would you play in the background?
- Would you volunteer or give back to community in any way?
- What new skill would you learn?
- Most importantly, how would this special day make you feel?

- Is this a feeling you want to experience more of in your life?
- Is this day achievable and realistic?
- Can you create this day within the structure of your current life? I'm hoping you give it an emphatic yes!

You now have created the Holy Grail Day on paper for yourself, and that's a pretty big deal in my book!

Let's stretch out this exercise and turn your perfect day into the perfect lifestyle! Would you do the same things or add some additional ingredients to your recipe? Do NOT allow yourself to feel guilty because you are indulging yourself. This is YOUR time, and nobody can tell you otherwise. Keep in mind what your overall lifestyle goals are while you're doing this.

Please write down all of it, either in your journal or on note cards. Everything from A-to-Z. Let your imagination run wild and your pen run out of ink.

- Where would you live?
- What kind of house would you have?
- What kind of car would you like to drive?
- Where would you go on vacation?
- What new projects or businesses would you start?
- What workshops or courses would you attend?
- What nonprofit or charity help would you like to do?
- How would you give back to your community in time and/or money?
- How much money would you set aside for retirement, second homes, college tuitions, a private jet, property in Montana, or whatever else you might want?

Allow yourself to have the creative freedom to authentically set these aspirations and goals. Unless you dream it, you'll never achieve it!

Ask yourself these and many more questions as you slowly create your masterpiece. Maybe you are already living the perfect life and that is very possible. To you, I say congratulations and a job well done! If not, we have a little more work to do. Make sure you are writing down your thoughts and answers.

Now the tough question. To make this life possible, what kind of income would you need to generate from your job, business, or both?

If you've already achieved this figure, congratulations! You are the proud owner of the perfect lifestyle and you didn't even know it. You are now one step closer to living the life of your dreams.

But if that number is beyond where you are now with your income, you'll need to reverse-engineer and restructure your business to attain your perfect life.

This is a book about putting value in your dreams, getting control of your time, and crafting a better life for yourself and your family while running a profitable business.

Now you have some guidelines for what you would like your life to look like from close range and from a distance.

Designing your perfect life can be one of the most enjoyable experiences you'll ever explore. It allows you to get to know yourself on an intimate level and will give your business a world-class jolt of adrenaline. It will not be easy by any stretch of your imagination, but that's why very few people are entrepreneurs.

I believe our ability to ask and work through difficult questions about how we view the world is an absolute must if we want to reap the benefits of thinking like a true UE.

First, envision and set your goals. Painting the masterpiece that is your life needs a healthy dose of creative thinking, followed by reverse-engineering your business and setting goals to help you achieve that vision. There is no quick fix that will give you the success you dream of, but there are simple questions you can ask yourself to shake the bushes and keep the cobwebs from creeping into your brain.

As we have discussed in detail, designing your perfect lifestyle is a matter of perspective and philosophy. It's much more than the car you drive, the house in which you live, or the amount of money in your 401k.

It's about gaining control over your precious time, so you can enjoy each special moment that comes your way without distractions.

It takes a very special person to keep their nose to the grindstone each day. My goal for you is that you'll begin to replace negative habits in your life with positive, productive habits that will ignite your dreams like never before. If you are a business owner, you know the joy of doing inventory at the end of each month.

POPCORN EXCERCISE

I call this the Popcorn Exercise. At the end of the process, you will have a firm grasp on everything that is inside of your Life Warehouse. The more information you have about yourself, the better equipped you will be to create the kind of life that you have always wanted.

We need to be acutely aware of who we are and what motivates us. That is why spending time with yourself is an important part of your daily routine. Grab a pen, a notepad, a good cup of coffee, and hit your back deck for a while.

You are going to break your life down into three categories: Personal, Family, and Professional. This exercise intends to get your life, as it exists today, onto a piece of paper:

Personal

- Do you get upset at yourself for not sticking to your diet and exercise program? Describe what your current diet and exercise routines are, then write a new plan with new routines you will begin.

- Are you satisfied with your spiritual growth? Do you attend church services as much as you would like? If you are not religious, do you budget adequate personal or alone time so you're in touch with your internal voice? Write out a plan for your personal development.

- What hobbies are you involved in? Do you spend as much time as you would like to participate in them? Write out a plan for what activities you would like to pursue.

- Have you given up some of your passions because of children or career? Would you want to make them part of your life again?

- What do you like about yourself? How can you improve on those things?

- What don't you like about yourself? How can you improve on those things?

The purpose of the Popcorn Exercise is to "rattle your brain" a little and remove the cobwebs. Once you have brainstormed about your life as it exists today, it's time to give some thought about where you want your life to be tomorrow and begin building your perfect lifestyle.

Brainstorm for a Breakthrough

You have already handcrafted your perfect lifestyle, so now it's time to set goals in order to make that happen. Grab a stack of 3x5 index cards and let the creative juices flow! You are going to write down your personal and professional goals for the next 12 months. Your personal goals should be done before the others. You started this process earlier, so it should be easy to add to your chicken scratches and notes.

Do you want to take a vacation this year? Do you have your eye on a special boat or set of golf clubs? How about your garden? Would you like to spend more time cultivating it or working in the yard?

What about other hobbies you haven't had time for recently? If it's important to you, then you should make the time in your schedule to read, write, paint, or play with the family dog.

Write down one goal per note card. What projects have you been meaning to start or finish? Where do you want to be in one month, three months, a year, or five years? What new hobbies do you want to learn? What old hobbies and interests would you like to bring back into your life? What projects have you been putting off because you just didn't have the time? Where do you want to go on vacation? What about your family? Would you like to spend more quality time with each of them individually? Write it all down on a note card. This is the next step towards designing your perfect lifestyle.

You may have an entire stack of things you've been meaning to get to but have not dedicated the necessary time.

This exercise must be done at a time and place where you won't be interrupted or distracted. By spending just fifteen minutes a day immersed in setting goals for your life and brainstorming, you will begin to create positive habits that will stick with you for the rest of your life. Once you come up with an idea, write it down. After you put it on paper, it will be much easier to expand the idea and develop it into creative breakthroughs.

Prioritize (The Salsa Box)

Now it's time to prioritize and organize your goals. If you tried to complete everything in your stack, I venture to say you would fail miserably and get disgusted with yourself in the process. Instead of eating the whole pizza all at once, you need to eat one slice at a time, so set some realistic goals.

Categorize your goals into three groups, similar to Level I, Level II, and Level III's perfect days. Goals or projects that you can't wait to get started on can be placed into the "hot" section of your salsa box. Items that are a little more long-term can be put into the "medium" category. Lastly, things that are long term, or possibly things you may never get to, can be put into the "mild" section.

Your "Salsa Box" goals will make it easier to establish some realistic timelines. By having everything already written down in your Salsa Box, you will increase your chances of success.

Share

If you want to truly make a difference in your life, you must become accountable to at least one other living person. It may be your spouse, your business partner, or your best friend, but it should be someone who understands and supports you. Set a time where you can lay out your game plan and share your goals and aspirations with them.

Ask the other person to make sure to hold your feet to the fire on occasion so you don't get lazy. If you set up a weekly conversation with them to discuss how things are going, you will allow the other person to be involved with your efforts in a very personal way.

Take Action

Once you have established your list of goals and shared them with a confidant, it's time to put your money where your mouth is. Putting some of your goals into motion can be a revolutionary step!

Don't make up excuses or come up with reasons why you can't do something. Just go and get it done.

As you put this program into action and begin to emulate passionate successful people, choose something small that you will be able to accomplish easily. Dedicate yourself to doing it every day for one week.

Maybe it's something as simple as going for a short walk at lunch, spending thirty minutes a day reading self-improvement books, working on sales projections for next quarter, going through boxes in your basement, or stopping on the way home to visit a friend who's been feeling down lately.

Once you begin to make these small items part of your daily routine, the bigger things won't seem quite so daunting and overwhelming. The smallest things can make the biggest difference.

Self-Doubt and Limited Ambition

Limited ambition is another obstacle to the UE life. Dreams should be just a little bit out of reach, but not out of sight. Otherwise, they wouldn't be dreams, would they? If your dreams exceed your self-image, you'll very likely do something stupid to sabotage that dream.

Earlier in my business life, I sabotaged many projects and got in the way of my own success. Ultimately, my self-doubt overwhelmed my desire to succeed. Once I learned to get out of my own way, my business fortunes changed.

Imagine that when you wake up tomorrow, everything you do will be done to the best of your ability. You'll give 110% effort to each activity you've planned for your day, disregarding any fears you may have. No obstacles. No negative thinking. No procrastination. Do you think this attitude will impact how your day turns out?

Resistance to Change

We're all creatures of habit, preferring to be comfortable with daily routines. Do you consider change wonderful and exciting, as long it's happening to someone else?

Life is in a constant state of flux, so we tend to gravitate towards our comfort zones. It seems too risky to try something new.

Comfort zones are neither good nor bad, but most people mistakenly think they perform their best when they are in a safe and familiar place.

I truly dislike being comfortable. If it gets to be too much, I'll create some chaos and shake up my world a bit. I get extremely bored with my life if my daily routines begin to feel "always the same." It drives me to the point at which I must either create a new product, start a new business, buy a new business, or completely shake up my routines.

No matter how enthusiastic you are, you'll stagnate if you don't take responsibility in your job, marriage, friendships, and hobbies. Anything not making progress is on its way to becoming stagnant and boring, which is to be avoided when pursuing and embracing our lives with passion as successful UEs.

Here are some exercises that can help shake the bushes of your life:

- Try a new restaurant this week. I challenge you to try a cuisine you're unaccustomed to.
- Buy different brands at the grocery store, such as deodorant, toothpaste, or dish soap.
- Take a new route to work. Be pleasantly surprised at how much beauty there is out there.

- Listen to a style of music you typically don't listen to. Scan your radio, download Amazon Music, or iHeartRadio.

- Sample a different dinner recipe for seven straight nights. Google and research recipes add the ingredients to your weekly shopping list. Give your culinary palate a shake up!

- Read a book completely out of your comfort zone.

- Switch the side of the bed you sleep on. You may have to sweet-talk your spouse or significant other, but you'll be amazed how different it makes you feel.

- If you have longer hair, try a different hairstyle or add some color.

- Pick an obscure subject you know very little about. Research and read about it, watch videos on it, then write a five hundred-word essay. Don't worry about making it sound like a Pulitzer prize-winning document; just pour your heart and effort into making it the best report you've ever written.

- Eat and write with your opposite hand for twenty-four hours. Don't worry about dropped spaghetti. Practice writing your name twenty-five times and see how much you can improve. This exercise activates the opposite side of your brain, rewarding you with a very powerful sensation after a short time. I try this technique two-to-three times a week, just to keep things a little off-centered.

- Instead of salting your food, try seasonings like salad dressings, hot sauces, pepper, BBQ sauces, vinegars, and spices for flavor. Make this a fun project and see what kinds of flavors stimulate your taste buds!

If you keep doing what you have always done, you'll keep getting what you've always gotten. It'll be virtually impossible to break out of your mental funk unless you shake up your mental branches to stimulate your foggy brain.

As Albert Einstein noted, *"We cannot solve our problems with the same thinking we used when we created them."*

Take a risk! You might not like it, but you'll never know unless you try.

If you step up to the plate, you might strike out. If you don't try, you'll never know the true joy of hitting a home run. Barry Bonds struck out over fifteen hundred times during his career, but he has also hit more home runs than anyone else in Major League Baseball history.

When you take a risk or face a fear, you move forward with your life. Eventually, you will become successful. As challenging as it may sound, this is a simple formula in living life to the fullest.

Here's another problem with comfort zones. If you're good, staying comfy can keep you from becoming great! That in and of itself should motivate you to get off your butt!

Lack of Discipline

Show me a successful businessperson, and I'll show you someone who is disciplined and dedicated to his or her mission. Success and failure are habits and self-fulfilling prophecies. If you don't prioritize and build positive habits, you will just stagnate and create your own demise.

In high school, I competed in the 400-meter dash on a national level and became an All-American. Between my coach, parents, friends, and competition, I was able to create a very strong set of goals I wanted to accomplish with my running. At one point, my times were on track to qualify for the U.S. Olympic Trials in Eugene, Oregon.

Unfortunately, a torn hamstring ended my college sprinting career, forcing me to retire long before I was ready.

But that experience left an indelible lifelong impact. Athletics is a powerful way to learn about self-discipline and setting goals. I know that my core values and beliefs are firmly rooted in the training I received from competitive sports.

Do you wait to see how you feel before making plans? Are you easily sidetracked, or do you have a sense of discipline? The key to staying focused and dedicated isn't hard if it's something you love and are passionate about.

Any discipline you desire must be built up gradually. If your goal is to run a marathon next year, you can't start out by running twenty-six miles on your first day of training. Start small and work your way up!

Fear

Our innate fear of trying something new has been part of human nature since the dawn of civilization. We tend to avoid any kind of risk if it has anything to do with taking us out of our comfort zone.

Fear stops many people from taking risks. If we aren't willing to walk out on a limb, we'll never get to the best fruit that the tree of life has to offer.

Overcoming our fear is how we learn to do just about everything in our lives, such as eating different foods for the first time, driving a car, talking to strangers, speaking up at meetings, or playing catch with our kids. They all come with certain levels of risk.

Trying a new variety of apple vs. investing $1,000,000 into a new business are both risky in their own unique ways. As humans, we like to take "measured" risks, meaning we can mitigate what may happen to us.

Pessimists and negative thinkers say things like, "You might get struck by lightning if you go outside," or "Did you know over one hundred people a day are killed in car wrecks in the US, which means I shouldn't drive?" Boy, what a waste of a person's great potential and mind space to think so negatively!

Nobody likes to lose, but there's no loss in going for it at all. The only loss in not trying is not having gone for it.

How do you overcome negative talk with yourself and people you meet? If you are unable to convince these people to be more open to having a positive outlook, then it's time to move on. Life is too short to allow yourself to be surrounded with people who attempt to bring you down, whether it's unintentional or not.

It's completely cool to surround yourself with people who espouse ideas opposite to yours. This can open your thinking to new ideas and creative problem solving. But negative thinking has no place in your 86,400-second day!

Setting Goals

In my business life, I am ruthless. I'm an extremely aggressive marketer, an above-average salesperson who knows how to close, and I find niches in the marketplace that are not being occupied by others. I know how to focus on my superpowers and squeeze out every drop of potential to win.

I delegate 80% of my daily tasks that brings only 20% of my results, leaving me with the 20% of my time to focus on the right tasks that bring 80% of my positive results. If you give me a brand-new business, I am confident that I will have that brand sailing towards the top of the food chain within six months. I would do this in part by offloading what I would call the second-tier activities, which allows me to focus on getting the biggest return on my time investment.

I temper this confident attitude with a much more subdued approach in my personal life. Because I am dedicated to having my perfect lifestyle at the top of the pyramid, it makes me more dedicated to getting my work done as quickly and efficiently as possible.

In looking back on my business journey, the takeaway for you should be to use common sense. If you have a laser-beam focus on your goals, priorities and time, you can revolutionize your business blueprint. My businesses are constrained by design. I have the mindset of a millionaire, but that doesn't mean that I must relinquish control over my life in order to attain that status.

Let's proceed with a simple exercise that will start defining some of your personal and professional goals, which will ultimately lead to the master plan for your perfect lifestyle. Don't worry about the money aspect for now. Just answer these questions honestly.

Be sure to write down your answers. Simply writing down your thoughts and goals is more effective in communicating with your subconscious to better achieve your aspirations.

Have fun playing and imagining your dream lifestyle.

If you had a magic wand:

- How many days off a week would you like?
- What will you do with your free time?
- Where would you like to travel?
- What hobbies would you like to spend more time on?
- What kind of car do you want to drive?
- What kinds of clothes do you want to wear?

- What kind of house do you want to live in?
- Which relationships are most important to you, and how can you nurture them?
- What would you change about yourself for self-improvement?

We'll call this perfect lifestyle list the Holy Grail since it contains all the shiny objects in the sky you'll always be striving for as a UE.

Now, here is the challenging part. You need to come up with a grand total dollar amount. How much will it take to comfortably sustain your vision for the Holy Grail? You have now started to paint a picture of your perfect lifestyle.

Deciding on what you want is the first step towards getting it. Our thoughts determine the direction of our lives. Life is more about the journey than the destination. If you change your thinking, you can change your life.

Harness Your Mental Power to Imagine Success

Imagine a big, juicy lemon sitting on the table in front of you. Grab a knife and cut it into wedges. With your mind's eye, smell the citrus wafting through the room. The refreshing scent fills the air with bursts of new energy to revitalize your senses. Still in your mind's eye, take a wedge, take a huge bite, and suck the wedge until all the juice is completely in your mouth. Very sour, isn't it?

Are you salivating? This is how the power of words affects and engages us emotionally. Words are simple tools that enable us to create dreams, including that amazing vision of where you want to be in your life.

Do you have a vision of how you want your life to be? Is your dream embedded in your brain in a way that is so compelling that it drives you to where you need to be? Is it as sensory as the cut lemon and refreshing aroma wafting through all your senses?

Your mind is an incredibly powerful tool in helping you achieve goals and grab your slices of happiness.

We've been taught to believe that our dreams are not meant to come true and that dreaming takes us away from tasks at hand. People accused of being daydreamers are thought to be lazy, foolish, or *"not plugged into reality."*

And yet, how would things have ever gotten done if we didn't imagine the results beforehand? If Thomas Edison had not tried, failed, and retried over 6,000 times, we would not have the benefit of electric light bulbs today.

Daydreaming is key to sharpening your focus on what you really want. Every invention and every great new idea were birthed at one time by people who daydreamed. I've been accused of being a daydreamer for much of my life, but I can honestly say that many of my "aha!" bright ideas have been the result of my mind being allowed to wander off into the great unknown.

Once upon a time, there was a man living in a cold cave who daydreamed about making fire to stay warm, but it took us over one million years to figure out how to utilize it. Someone daydreamed about inventing ice cream over four thousand years ago, but it wasn't until only over a hundred years ago that someone came up with the idea for the ice cream cone. In 1775, the flush toilet was invented, followed eighty-two years later by the invention of toilet paper!

The world goes around because of people who daydreamed, imagined, and strongly believed they could make the world a better place for themselves and others.

You're never too young or too old to dream big dreams. Figure out what's holding you back from designing the life of your dreams and then forge ahead.

Taking Responsibility

We all have times in which we feel like the world is out to get us. I remember events in my life when it seemed everything I was doing didn't turn out as planned, regardless of how hard I tried. I felt I was doing the right things with the right amount of effort, but the dice just didn't roll my way.

Looking back at every one of my failures, I can say with 110% certainty that the reason I failed was because of my attitude and my effort.

There was a time in my life when I made terrible financial decisions, leading to my filing for bankruptcy back in the early 1990s. It was a difficult lesson, but one I wouldn't trade for anything in the world. Without this failure, I wouldn't have been able to lay the groundwork for future successes and accomplishments. I had to take responsibility for my bad decisions and live with the consequences.

Hitting the bottom does teach us many lessons, one of which is not wanting to be there ever again!

Potential alone isn't enough. Taking responsibility is the match that sets passion ablaze. We must have a better attitude in life so passion can arise from the depths of our guts to fill out every cell of our being. Conversely, a bad, negative, and pessimistic attitude kills passion and needs to be exterminated ASAP.

Uncaring people with bad attitudes are always unhappy and they can't understand why. Do you know anyone with that kind of mentality? If this is you, YOU NEED TO STOP.

To live the life of a UE, you must avoid becoming stagnant,

inactive, and prevent yourself from getting a terminal case of "bad attitude." If you've lost the joy on your life's journey, maybe it's because you've allowed a bad attitude to creep into your headspace. You must take responsibility, however unconsciously it may have occurred.

Attitude is much more important than your background, education, money, failures, successes, or what other people think, say, or do. If all but one of the strings on your guitar is broken, then all you can do is play on that one string that's left: your attitude. Life is 5% what happens to us, and 95% how we react to it.

How prepared are you to meet adversity? What percentages would you use to describe how you react to circumstances?

Moreover, it's very easy for entrepreneurs to fall into that old management trap of getting caught up in the daily grind of managing our businesses. It sucks up the energy, time, and motivation to enjoy happy moments we feel we're owed, such as daydreaming.

Managing employees, refining your website SEO, crafting your social media posts, keeping up with marketing and promotions, cleaning the bathroom, mowing the lawn, and doing the books can be too rigorous for one person. Before we know it, we're working sixteen hours a day, week after week. For what?

Private Time

Spending time with nobody else around is the foundation of all successful entrepreneurs, regardless of what industry they are involved in. Without private time, you will find it impossible to realize your full potential and set yourself on the path that leads to the proper work/life balance.

When I need a jolt of creative electricity, I go to the mountains in Montana. Simple things like listening to the sounds of the wind dancing through the tall trees, watching the morning mist rise from the wet grass and river, and building a campfire with while having a good cup of coffee are euphoric and revitalizing to me.

There are trees and rivers in every corner of the country, but Montana has a special power over my soul. Pat and my mother bought property there back in the 1990s. It is a nurturing place where I feel most at home, regardless of where I live.

Mother Nature is the battery for my soul. I can easily get in touch with myself very quickly in her midst. Regardless of what is going on in my life, she always puts things back in order and gives me the proper perspective to solve many of life's challenges. Where do you go to recharge?

Life's Great Lesson

One day, a millionaire businessman took his son to the country to show him how the poor folks lived. They spent a few days on a farm with an extremely poor family. After they returned home, the father asked his son what he thought of his experience.

"It was great, Dad," the son replied. *"Did you see how poor some people in this world are?"* the father asked.

"I sure did. I saw that we have a dog, and they have four. We have a big pool in our backyard, and they have a lake and a stream running through theirs that has no end. In our garden, we have fancy imported Italian oil lamps, and they have a sky filled with the stars. Our patio reaches all around to our front porch, and they have the entire horizon. Thank you, Dad, for showing me what true riches are."

Some people think that their value as a human being comes from working long hours, driving big expensive cars, dropping fifty thousand dollars on a vacation, and having lots of bling.

Me, I'm more of a BBQ on the back deck, guitar in the corner, hanging out in the mountains, reading a good business book, and playing with my kids. That's not to say that I don't enjoy the finer things in life, but we all need to stick to our core values and beliefs.

Designing and creating your perfect lifestyle may take some serious brainstorming and redefining what is truly important, and some rearranging of your current priorities. You may need to completely break things down into the absolute smallest pieces, then rebuild your thinking with fewer moving parts. Realizing your dream life is not a 1-time thing, it's a living and breathing organism that requires constant attention and mental energies.

Once that piece of the puzzle is on solid ground it's time to work on your business blueprint.

CHAPTER 2

Effective Time Management

I believe that each one of us wishes we had more time in our days. On Friday afternoon, we are filled with excitement about all the wonderful things we will accomplish on the weekend, then Sunday night rolls around and we wonder where the weekend went.

There are two types of people on this planet: Those who squander their time, and those who make every second count.

The first type simply waits for the time to pass. For them, the time-lapse is often an annoyance they simply can't wait to end. The example is anxiously waiting for the working hours to pass.

The second type makes every passing second to count, instead of just waiting for the sand to slip through the narrow funnel, they live with almost a pathological intent and never allow time to pass unnoticed. For them, time-lapse is a living process and they always strive to be active participants in it.

Effective time management is the one thing that separates top performers from the herd and allows them to reach higher ground.

There's a profound difference between time management and not caring about anything else beyond the current interest. And while we've developed a neat way to track time, it's beyond our capabilities to absolutely control it. We can, however, induce a certain, necessary level of control over the chaos of our lives. This means controlling our most precious asset, time, to our best abilities.

We cannot earn more of it or save it as we do with money or commodities. It is slipping away with every breath we take. The only thing we can do, in between our breaths, is controlling how and on what we are spending that time.

The 80/20 Principle

When you choose to stay focused on one single task at a time, you invariably end up cutting out some things you enjoy that may not be bearing fruit. We will do an exercise to help you eliminate, automate, or delegate up to 80% of your daily tasks and free your time and energy to dedicate to your superpowers.

Most people have heard of the 80/20 principle, which suggests that 80% of your outcomes are from 20% of your efforts. Conversely, 20% of your outcomes are from the other 80% of your efforts. The point here? Identifying a group of top priorities and then staying focused on them should be your number one focus. I want you to think about what activities in your day produce the most amount of positive results in your business or personal life.

Earlier in my entrepreneur career, I made a living in the world of professional photography, travelling the world teaching the finer points of business. Today, it seems like everybody and their brother's friend's aunt's sister is now a "photographer," which has put a big crunch on those who have been professionally trained. Weekend warriors and soccer moms have taken the industry by storm with their $500 cameras and smartphones.

Professional photographers are slaves to their computers and workflows. Image processing that used to be handled by professional color labs are now being done by the photographers themselves, adding significantly more hours to their already long work week.

In photography, only three things make money: shooting, selling, and marketing. That's it! Retouching a digital file doesn't fall under any of those categories, but this digital process is consuming many pros. Why? Because they think it saves money, and they know how to do it. A deadly combination.

It's easy for us to dispose of things we dread and despise, but what about the things we're attached to? This makes it a lot harder because our emotions are involved. Photographers who spend eight hours on a Sunday editing and retouching files from Saturday's wedding are attached to an outdated method of running a business. In the open market, the job of a digital retoucher is $15-$20/hour. If a professional photographer were asked if they would be willing to work for $15-$20/hour, they would laugh in your face! Well, if they are doing their own retouching…

Instead of outsourcing the job to someone to free up their valuable time, they choose to do it themselves because they're emotionally attached to the digital process or mistakenly think they're saving money.

In small business today, there are 3 levels of 'Time Value"-

- $15-$20/hr.- the tasks that keep your business moving forward like answering the phone, responding to e-mails, processing orders, assembling products, etc.…
- $50/hr.- the day-to-day management of your business, setting sales goals and objectives, personnel management and training, etc...
- $500/hr.- constructing the long-range goals of the company, creating the broad strokes, and crafting the overall vision. This is where *YOU* should be spending most of your precious time.

I can tell you this without any hesitation. Doing $15-$20 worth of work per hour is NOT what business owners should be doing with their time, whatever industry they're in!

Do you have a list of tasks that can be delegated or eliminated from your routine? Think about that.

This way of thinking may be challenge the way you're used to running your business, but I can tell you your business will be revolutionized by quantum leaps if you begin to entertain the idea of redesigning your thought processes.

The POD System

The way I do it is with what I call the POD system. Every activity is entered into a category, assigned a block of time, and placed on your schedule.

One trick that I always do is at the end of each week is to sit down and plan the following week. I have some things that are in my schedule book for weeks and months in advance, but the day-to-day tasks that are necessary to keep the ship afloat are where the ultimate success lies.

On Monday morning, I have my game plan already in place and can be much more productive than simply allowing the wind to dictate where my time is spent.

For example, the first two hours of my day are always *"Mitche time."* This includes listening to music or a podcast, reading a book, drinking a good cup of coffee, and reviewing my goals for the day.

This POD of time is circled in my schedule book. I don't allow anything to interrupt me during this time. I make sure I do not get distracted by email, texts, social media timelines or notifications, and so on.

It's very important that this first POD of the day be completely controlled by you and that you're not reacting to anything the world is dishing out.

In the Family POD, I get the kids fed, ready, and bussed off to school. After that, the Reactive POD consists of replying to emails, returning phone calls, and anything else the world needs from me.

In the Revenue POD, I have a pre-defined list of objectives written down ahead of time.

After this work POD, it's back to either a personal or family POD to finish off the day. If you were to look at my schedule book, you would see a series of blocked out sections that are dedicated time slots for that activity. I'm not successful all the time, but I've developed a strong sense of purpose when it comes to sticking to my guns over the years.

This strategy is dependent upon asserting your ability to keep outside influences from interrupting you. If you're in the middle of your personal POD, don't spend time on your phone looking at work emails or checking online orders. If you're in your Revenue POD, don't allow yourself to be distracted by checking your Facebook timeline or looking up a recipe for tonight's dessert.

It's like putting out a virtual *"DO NOT DISTURB"* sign around your brain, then working like crazy to stay on the course. Always keep in mind the "nagging "question: Does this activity or task help me attain my ultimate lifestyle goals? Utilize the POD System, in a scheduling app and don't forget to limit their duration. Continue by adding everything else you might plan for that day.

In the evening, take a few moments and rewind your day. See what you've missed. See what you've miscalculated. Understand your routine. Recall all those seemingly insignificant events you failed to predict that caused time losses. After a while, you'll start noticing how a vast number of such events repeat themselves day after day. In order to become a master of your schedule, you will need to be laser-focused on the most important tasks that bring the biggest results...Your own 80/20 list.

Delegate, Eliminate, Automate

Meet my long-time friend Bob, an entrepreneur who started out doing things the hard way, but then turned smart instead. We'll use him as a real-life example of how a single man can disrupt a global paradigm.

Just like you, Bob always dreamed of owning his own business. Eventually, he quit his job and invested some money starting his professional lawn care company. He purchased a new lawnmower, rakes, wheelbarrows, gloves, and other items needed to be successful with his new venture. At that point, Bob was the only employee and in charge of not only mowing all the lawns, but also marketing, networking, sales, website design, payables, and other tasks.

To his own surprise, Bob managed to pick up several clients over a short time and eventually nearly filled up his schedule with recurring jobs every week. Not bad for a new business, but Bob knew how to work hard and smart.

One day, he received a call from the local shopping mall asking if he'd be interested in taking over the contract for their landscape maintenance.

After meeting with management, Bob figured that he would need to spend nearly all his time during the week at the mall just to fulfill the contract. That meant that all his other clients would have to wait.

On the flip side, the contract would exactly double his weekly revenue, so Bob had a hard time with the decision. Let's say there is a big hopper or vat that has three different sections: Delegation, Elimination, and Automation.

For the sake of the argument, let's put Bob's new opportunity into the hopper.

- Can Bob **delegate** the job to someone else? He could potentially hire a new employee to handle only the mall contract or handle private residence contracts. That's certainly a possibility.
- Can he simply turn down the contract and **eliminate** the possibility altogether? Absolutely. But it depends on what Bob's ultimate goals are for growing his business.
- Can he streamline and **automate** the task? Bob could purchase a larger lawnmower allowing him to finish his jobs much quicker, thus freeing up valuable time to handle more work. Great possibility!

When Bob sat down to look at all his options, he remembered that his ultimate goal was to expand his business and hire employees, thus giving him more time to grow the business.

Most importantly, this strategy would give him more time to spend with his family.

Hence, Bob decided to bring on another employee and purchased a bigger lawnmower to handle the larger jobs. This freed up more time and allowed him to pick up five more commercial contracts.

The bottom line is, simply asking straightforward questions can potentially revolutionize your business. Therefore, give yourself the creative freedom and passion to think out-of-the-box. You'll be amazed at what can transpire!

Today, Bob lives and works his version of the 24/7 Lifestyle, and just like you should, he loves every moment of it.

The 4X Formula

By automating, delegating and eliminating your daily tasks in an uber-efficient way, you will be able to free up a substantial amount of time in your day. This time can be re-invested into the 20% of your tasks that bring you 80% of your positive results, or can be spent doing other things, your choice.

Basically, you will be able to get twice as much done in ½ the amount of time. I called this "4Xing" your life! It's a very straight forward and simple formula but one that will require constant attention if you are going to become a master.

The 1st Component- MENTAL IMAGERY

Mental imagery is a neat mind trick that enables us to predict up to 90% of events, hours, days, weeks, and years ahead. In other words, it allows you to plan to perfection even over the large time gaps. It's something frequently used by top athletes, military strategists, and top executives. How does it work?

When he was still a young athlete, Olympic gold-medalist Michael Phelps had real difficulties concentrating. He was built for the swimming pool but didn't yet have a champion mentality. A long, flat torso with long and strong arms on relatively short legs made him exceptionally hydrodynamic. But his inability to focus frustrated Phelps.

To solve this severe issue, his trainer designed a two-part mental workout that would ultimately make Michael Phelps the fastest swimmer in the world.

In the first phase, Michael was tasked to memorize every moment of the training and then rewind the mental movie afterward. Day after day, Phelps would teach his brain to remember more and more details about strokes, turns, energy levels, and duration. In less than six months, Phelps was capable of remembering details. He was even able to analyze the dynamics with surgical precision.

Then came phase two where Michael was supposed to plan his own training ahead of time, using his memories as the foundation. Once on the edge of a swimming pool, Phelps would play the mental movie and then jump in the water.

With practice, he learned to accurately assess the duration of the race, down to the second. His brain would calculate the needed energy investment for every stroke so he could perfectly balance the reserves. Only a year after, Phelps became the fastest male swimmer in his age category. Three years later, he broke several world records and won his first gold medal.

Phelps' secret, to a large extent, was the ability of the human brain to act as a learning machine. Just as you can develop a habit, you can teach your brain to execute complex tasks basically on autopilot. Those tasks soon transform into habits.

The 2nd Component – IVY LEE METHOD

So many young executives are bragging about their multitasking abilities. There must be something to it, right?

Only chaos, confusion, and underachieving. Multitasking and micromanaging are the two capital mistakes in business operations. To an experienced eye, they are indicating an inexperienced person or, at the very least, someone who's biting far more than he's capable of chewing.

Multi-taskers experience frequent burnouts, which negatively affects their overall efficiency.

Back in the 1920s, one man developed the single most efficient method of prioritizing that is, in its original state, in use even today.

Ivy Lee was hired to coach the executives of American Steel magnate Charles M. Schwab. Lee advised Schwab's managers to list only six tasks for the following day according to their priorities. They were expected to work on completing those tasks in the allotted time without proceeding to the next task unless the current one was finished. Today, most successful managers are using Ivy Lee's Method of prioritizing when creating a schedule.

Why only 6? And what happens if we fail to execute all six

planned for a given day? You simply move the unfinished tasks to the next day and fill in the remaining spots until there are exactly six tasks.

"Following this simple practice creates the most important trait of every efficient businessman: Focus"

There's only so much you can fit into a single working day and still maintain a high level of quality. If you often find yourself in a situation where there are more than six tasks to complete, which probably indicates that you're micromanaging. Six is the sweet spot. Simple as that. If you were to compare your list of 6 things, I bet it would be very close to the 80/20 exercise you did earlier!

Now, imagine the combo of mental imagery and Ivy Lee's Method of prioritizing in planning anything you can think of, especially time management…

The 3rd Component- PRACTICAL APPLICATION

The biggest challenge in time management is not planning and organizing a schedule, it's dealing with time vampires that chip away at your list of priorities and by wasting vast amounts of minutes and hours of your day. Some of this is not our fault, but most of it is. We make decisions throughout our day that allows our focus to broken, and our important tasks delayed.

Two Types of Schedules

One manages your private life. The other manages professional tasks. Here's the trick.

Tasks must be organized in a way that allows a so-called, power-scheduling. We'll do a little exercise soon to teach you what power-scheduling truly is.

Now, the key here is not merely listing tasks. You also need to limit the duration of each task to preserve time. If you are having a scheduled meeting, that event must have both start and end time and you shouldn't exceed it unless necessary.

That's what makes Ivy Lee's Method so powerful. Once you get used to it, it will become increasingly easy to ditch everything that has lower significance in terms of a priority.

This is also the moment when that thin line between alleged "time management" and just not caring is crossed. Another brilliant feature of Ivy Lee's Method.

Sometimes an idea may occupy your entire being. It becomes virtually impossible to shake it off. What do you do in such a situation?

"Sometimes, following instincts rather than blindly obeying a pre-programmed schedule returns far better results"

EXERCISE: Power-Scheduling

Power-Scheduling refers to creating and managing a private schedule and a professional one. How do you do it efficiently?

By combining mental imagery, and Ivy Lee's Method of prioritizing.

Close your eyes for a couple of minutes and visualize the day ahead. Direct a mental movie of your day.

Start by imagining well-known fixed time events. Remember, there's only so much that you can't predict when you put your mind into it. For the most part, your days are following the same rut that is, again, based on a set of habits you developed over the course of time. Your habits simply fit in those of your private and professional environments.

I truly believe that if you focus on the most important tasks, while either automating, delegating or eliminating everything else, you will completely revolutionize the way your business operates. You will suddenly find that you have extra time in your day, and from there you can choose what to do with it.

Perhaps invest it back into growing your business, looking for new opportunities, or taking your family on a picnic. The sky is the limit!

CHAPTER 3

High-Voltage Branding

I want to take you on a journey to a place where everything is perfect, where there is no stress or worry, and the streets are made of cheese. It's a place where you can buy anything, do anything, and be anything you want to be. This place is called your mind, and it is the most powerful tool we have been given.

Imagine it's a beautiful, warm Saturday afternoon in the fall, and you decide to go for a drive in the country. With all the hustle and bustle of everyday life, you don't get this opportunity as much as you would like, but today is your day. As you drive along, you decide to head over to a nearby lake that is known for its vibrant fall colors, and tranquil silence. Along the way, you notice that the leaves on the trees next to the road and on the hillside are slowly beginning to softly fall to the ground, as they create a bed of color on the pavement in front of you. With the window down, you can feel the wind tickling your face and you can smell the mustiness of fall. The sun is directly in front of you, and as the sun hits your face, you feel the warmth of its touch.

It's a feeling you crave and relish, and you want to soak up as much of this feeling as possible before the season passes, and winter digs in. You come to the road that will take you to the lake, and you take notice of the fact there are no other cars on the road coming or going……. The road is yours. You begin to feel the excitement of being at the lake by yourself and soaking up all it has to offer.

As you approach the lake, you find a place to park your car, and you begin the short walk down to the lake. You are about 100 yards or so from the bank, and you notice two little stores next to the road… one on the left, and one on the right. Your eyes first are attracted to the rustic-looking brown building on the right. You notice the broken rain gutter that is filled with moldy leaves from last season, and the grass hasn't been cut for quite some time.

There is a bike lying on its side in front, and you can tell it has seen better days…. The handlebars are covered with rust, and several of the spokes are missing from the rear tire. The dark brown paint that is around the windows and door is beginning to chip from age, and there are a couple of spiders that have made their home in the upper corner. The sign above the door reads…. Lakeside QuikMart. The smaller sign in the window above the spider web reads: Lemonade .50 cents and cookies - 10 for a dollar.

Your eyes then meander to the little white building on the other side of the road. There are bright red geraniums neatly planted in oak barrels that are placed along a cobblestone walkway leading up to the front entrance. The white picket fence the surrounds the entire building has tulips all around, and a Post Office box in the shape of a Trout sits atop a cast iron stake. On top of the building, a freshly painted sign reads "Heaven on Earth Country Store" with beautiful blues and greens and yellow throughout…. And then on a smaller sign below, the words, "Where Friends Meet." It almost makes you feel like you are at Grandma's house when you were little…safe, kind, and friendly.

You notice a small sign in the window that says, "Hand-squeezed Country Style lemonade made fresh this morning… only $2.00 a glass. Your mouth begins to water as you imagine drinking that glass of hand-squeezed Country Style fresh lemonade. The side windows are cracked open just enough that you can smell the fresh chocolate chip cookies that must have just pulled out of the oven only 10 seconds before. You would pay just about anything to have a bite of one of those cookies right now.

You pause for a moment, and glance at the brown building on the right side of the road, and then you glance back to the white building on the left side… You must make a choice of which place to go. Hmmm…Your mind is made up. You are going to ________.

Was there really any doubt as to which business you were going to go into? I don't think so. It didn't matter that the price was more, did it? It came down to the image that each business created in your mind…. And once that impression is made, it's virtually impossible to change how we feel.

The QuikMart may have had the best cookies in the world, but they sure didn't create much desire on our part to give them a try, for any price. The same process happens with your business. Judgments are made about you long before you speak the first words to a prospect.

I have always viewed branding as the cornerstone of all my businesses, regardless of the industry they are in. It's one of those things that you either absolutely are in love with or view it as a necessary evil in your business.

Regardless of your opinion, there is 1 absolute fact… "Your BRAND will determine if you are around in 1 year, 5 years, or 10 years from now."

Crush it and your odds are exponentially increased. Drop the ball and you will be a corpse on the side of the business highway.

Did you know that we as human beings make judgments of people, businesses, food, and other products within 5 seconds? 5

seconds. That sure doesn't give us much time before a decision has been made about how a potential customer feels about us, and what kind of value they believe us to have. You must always be prepared to be judged.

Marketing, positioning and image creation are much more than Facebook ads and direct mail pieces. It's the expression of who you are and what you do. It's all about what you wear, how you look, the way you walk and talk, the way you communicate with the rest of the world. It's as much about essence, as it is substance.

Most of us have been working our entire career trying to figure out the magic of branding and marketing and are met with great amounts of frustration. We become PhD's from the School of Hard Knocks, with a Minor in Adversity. We are constantly trying to reinvent the wheel instead of looking outside the box for the answers. Usually there is a simple answer for most obstacles.

Man's discovery of fire was huge, but it took us over 1 million years for us to figure out how to utilize it. Did you know ice cream was invented over 2000 years BC... but it wasn't until only 100 years ago someone came up with the idea for the ice cream cone. In 1775, the flush toilet and in 1857, 82 years later, toilet paper arrived!

We are surrounded with simple solutions to help us succeed. We just don't always see them. And some of the simplest things we normally don't even think about are right in front of our nose, yet we can't see the forest through the trees. Creating a positive image is done in much the same way. The things that make the biggest difference are the littlest of things.

Having a positive image will not only assure your survival in difficult times, it will also allow you to outshine your competition and prosper, even in tough times, because you will be one of the only people in your market place who markets smart. PT Barnum used to say he knew that half of all the money he spent on advertising was wasted, if you could just figure out which half....

You can avoid costly mistakes by learning from other people's mistakes or from borrowing valuable lessons from other industries. There is nothing wrong with that. You should study the leaders in your industry and in others and see what it is that gives them the competitive edge.

When you do things the same old way, you should expect the same old results. If you hit your head up against a wall and it gives you a headache... *STOP DOING IT!* You need to spend time observing and studying the most successful and innovative people. We will take you step by step through this process with the 5-second Image Challenge a little bit later.

As businesspeople and entrepreneurs, we make mistakes every day, but the most successful people in any industry are the ones who learn quickly from those mistakes and make the necessary changes to prevent those mistakes from happening again. "They fail fast and move on."

5 Biggest Business Mistakes

When it comes down to our branding efforts, most of our mistakes fall within 5 areas:

1) Failure to Have a Well Thought Out Marketing Plan - Anyone can captain the ship when the seas are calm. However, a good marketing plan does its best work when the seas are anything BUT calm. 80% of all businesses do not have any form of marketing plan at all... and 80% of all businesses aren't around in 5 years. Do you think this is just a coincidence? We have 2 jobs: 1 - to manage our customers and 2 – to market. Everything else is secondary.

2) Failure to Have A Clearly Defined Hook or Message - Without it, you are just a me too, an also ran, another run-of-the-mill

business. You will not become successful simply because you are the best. Da Vinci was dead for over 200 years before he became famous. I don't know about you, but I don't want to wait that long!

You need to know what it is that makes you special and unique in your marketplace. What is it that customers can't get from anyone else but you? What is your compelling reason that customers should come to your business instead of all others in your industry? Again, the numbers speak for themselves - 80% of all businesses couldn't tell you what their hook is, if asked. Are you one of the 80%, or do you want to be part of the 20% who make a difference?

3) Failure to Have Professional-Looking Marketing Pieces - It's all about first impressions. Everything you do must match your image. If you want to be known for BMW quality, then everything you do should be consistent with that goal.

4) Failure to Project Your Sales and Goals into the Future- We discussed this in detail in Chapter 1.

If it's important enough to you, you will figure out a way to make it happen. If you really want it to happen, and you take the necessary steps to accomplish it, it will happen - guaranteed. If you want to increase your gross income for the remainder of the year, you had better start making those plans and projections today. You need to price your products and services to allow for costs, overhead, and that 4-letter word - Profit.

With 4 out of 5 businesses being out of business in less than 5 years, making sure you have a thorough understanding of your cost breakdown on your products, and how much profit is generated from each sale? How many of your products will you need to sell, or what number of service calls will you need to perform in order to achieve your financial and personal goals? What do you want to make this year, and next year, and the year after that?

The biggest problem in most industries isn't that businesses are priced to cheaply, it's that we they are afraid to charge what they are worth.

If you would like to eliminate a certain segment of the business you currently do, then start making a game plan today. Figure out how you can smoothly exit that market and replace it with sales from your more lucrative types of customers. In order to truly focus, you must do LESS. You can practice hand grenade marketing.... Throw a bunch of stuff out there and hope it hits the target.... Or you can use laser beam marketing and hit only what you want.

The old saying.... "If you want to attract a .99 cent customer, get 1 .99 cent customer because if they like you, they will tell all their other .99 cent friends, which means you will have a bunch of .99 cent customers."

If you do a professional job and remember the value and power of the all mighty referral, they come to you already sold.

They understand your quality, your process and your pricing. If a customer comes to you and says, "My neighbor showed me their whatsahoosit, and I absolutely love it, and I want to get one for myself...and oh yea... they said they only spent .99 cent.... I can't wait." Your pricing strategy is an integral part of your brand, so it's something to be aware of.

It is just like the Lakeside QuikMart store example. It's going to take an awful lot of convincing to get us to spend even .50 cents on a glass of lemonade, or a buck on 5 cookies... Now, there is profit in the .99 cent customer, but you need to sell to a lot more of them than you do the $10, $100, or $1000 customer.

"It all comes down to what are your goals in life. Sometimes you are better off going fishing then taking a job that doesn't help you achieve your ultimate objectives and goals."

It's difficult to turn down business at first, but in the long run it will be healthier for your business and yourself. Let's face it...some customers are just not worth having. You have the ultimate say in how you spend your time.

Do you remember when it was you started disliking snakes, or spiders, or flying, or seafood, or asparagus? You may not remember a specific incident, but I bet you are acutely aware of the things in life you do and don't like. Most of those precepts, or beliefs, were embedded deep in our psyche from experiences that lasted 5, 10, maybe 15 seconds. Those precepts have been branded into your brain, which is where the term comes from.

When I was younger, I didn't like asparagus and couldn't tell you why or what it tasted like. I just knew I didn't like it. When I became an adult, I had the opportunity to have some with a meal, and didn't want to be rude, so I scooped up a serving...... and believe it or not, I liked it! I couldn't remember the time I decided asparagus was to be put on my list of things I didn't care for, but my subconscious mind had made up its mind. I'm sure you can think of several things in life you don't like, but can you remember when your dislike began?

The same dynamic happens when we are exposed to people and businesses. That very first impression infiltrates our mind and a judgment is made very quickly. In business, those judgments can either mean future success, or ultimate failure.

The 5-Second Image Challenge

Now, we are going to dive into what I call the 5-Second Image Challenge. As human beings and consumers, we make mental judgments in our minds daily. Right or wrong, within 5 seconds of seeing, feeling, hearing, smelling, or tasting something. We decide in our subconscious minds whether we like something. Those judgments can stay with us our entire lives in many cases.

We are going to be taking a close look at every aspect of what your business looks like, sounds like and feels like to a potential customer or an existing one. This is going to take an objective perspective, so if you think it would be better to have someone else along for the ride, feel free to ask your spouse, a close friend, or even a customer of yours if they would like to help out. We tend to become subjective observers of our business, and for this exercise we want you to be able to step out of your shoes, and into the shoes of that exact customer you want to attract.

Before we can begin looking into your business with an objective frame of mind, let's go see how other top-notch businesses handle this issue and expose ourselves to the best quality out there.

Take a couple of hours on a Saturday or Sunday afternoon, and take a trip to the local mall where the elite stores are located. Nike, Ralph Lauren, Polo, Bath & Body Works, Apple Genius Bar - any of these types of stores. Take a notepad with you so you can write down anything that strikes your fancy.

Notice their signage on the outside of the building, the colors and fonts they use for their logo, the smells as you walk in the front door, the overhead music that's playing, the way they have their displays organized, and what types of products are in those displays, the fonts they use on the header cards, the style of the carpet beneath your feet, the color of the walls, the items around the cash registers...colors and smells affect our emotions in a very big way. Once you have a good handle on your environment, look at the people who are shopping there.

What type of clothes are they wearing? What style of shoes do they have on? What about their hairstyles, age range, the color of the woman's purses, or the brand of the men's jeans? Notice the model of cars that are in the parking lot, and what colors seem to be the most popular. Anything about their customers you can identify - put it on paper. If you see something that will work great for you, write it down.

Stop by a nice art gallery, or a fine furniture store, or maybe stop into one of the upscale photography studios in your area. Make the same mental notations about what you observe there.

"There are plenty of great branding and marketing ideas we can find just by looking around at the world around us"

After spending a couple of hours going in and out of several stores of this class, drive yourself over to the local department store such as Wal-Mart, K-mart, or the local 5 and dime. Make the same observations about their business as you did with the first set of businesses. What impressions do you get from looking at the outside of their building?

How do their logos and signs compare to those of the first set of businesses? When you walk in the front door, do you get the same sense of quality and value? How are the displays arranged, and how are the prices advertised? What about the people shopping there? Do they have the same style of shoes, and the same models of cars? Walk around the store a bit and get a real good sense of who it is they want to attract into their building with their branding. It won't take you long to grasp what the marketing plan is of the big discount stores. High volume, low price, load 'em up, move 'em in, move 'em out! Yee-Haw!

This exercise should also be done online as well. Spend some time studying websites of the elite brands as well as the not-so-elite ones. You will notice subtle differences that separate them all.

The Perfect Customer

What does your perfect customer look like? Is it someone who shops at a high-end boutique and pays with an AmEx card, someone who shops at the warehouse stores, or is it a combination of both? Remember that there is a difference between the type of customer you may have today, and the customer you want for tomorrow. It's all part of knowing what you want out of life, and your business.

Once this step is completed, go back to your business, and spend a few minutes reviewing the observations you just made. Now, it's on to step 2 of the process which we are going to break down into 3 categories

1) Telephone Skills Inventory
2) Physical Inventory
3) Marketing Inventory

Telephone Skills Inventory

The goal of every effective marketing campaign is, ultimately to make the phone ring, right?

"And if you can't drive the prospect to your website or to pick up the phone and call you, all the marketing in the world is useless"

Do you know how much it costs to make the phone ring, or how much is costs to drive a prospect to your website? Here's an easy way to get a pretty good idea:

If you track each call that comes into your business already, this will be easy for you. If you don't, you will need to track every call that comes in for a period, let's say a week. Of course, calls from your family, friends, and the pizza delivery shop don't count.

Then, take the total number of calls you received and divide it into your marketing total expenses for the same period. You might be surprised by the amount. I've heard of numbers as low as $3, and as high as $1,100. You can also take the number of calls and divide it into your total sales for that period, which will give you a roundabout dollar amount that each call generated. It's not an exact science, but it will give you an idea of where you are.

The first thing you want to do is to listen to your voicemail message. This ought to be fun. I bet if I did a survey of 100 businesses around the country and had them write down what they say on their answering machine, it would sound something like this....

"Hello, and thanks for calling, if you've reached this message during normal hours, we are either with a customer, on the other line, or away from the office. Please leave us your name and number and we will give you a call back when we return. Thank you - and have a nice day.

Am I close? Don't worry... it's not just people in your industry that do that... it's all of America. Do you think people get tired of listening to the same old thing every time they call a business? Why not add a little pizzazz to the mix? For example, add some funny clown music in the background, share some enthusiasm, sincerity, and some excitement in your voice. Here is a good example:

"Hi, this is BoBo the clown from BoBo's Clown School, and I'm really glad you called. If you are calling to register for clown school, press 1, if you are calling to tell me I won the lottery, press 2, if you're my wife, I'll be home for dinner by 6. If you're the taxman, you called the wrong number! Hang up and do not pass go, do not collect $200! Thanks for calling Bobo's Clown School and make it a Clowntageous DAY."

For a clown school, something over the top like that would probably fit their image well, but I'm guessing that your business will fit somewhere along the spectrum between a Clown School and a Mont Blanc pen boutique.

There are several things you should pay attention to when listening to your message. Does it sound far away and tinny? Is there the proper enthusiasm in the voice? Is it sincere? Are the words spoken clearly and concisely into the speaker, or do the words run together and sound rushed?

There is nothing worse than calling another business and having the person on the message sound bored, irritated, and disgusted, like it was a bother for them to answer the phone. It makes me not want to do business with them. You can tell the businesses you want to do business with by the way their voicemail sounds. Make your message friendly, and spirited, and welcoming. This is something you can do right now, if you so choose. Grab a piece of scratch paper, write out your script, and put a new message on your message. You can put me on pause, I'll wait.

Then we have the live person answering the phone.... (Nasally sound) (Ring, Ring) "This is ABC Plumbing, home of the $49 septic tank extravaganza - how may I direct your call?"

You want to sound approachable, trustworthy, professional, and glad to be alive! Good Morning or Good afternoon, or Good evening, or Happy Holidays, or Happy New Year! This is Mitche, how can I help you today? If you use your first name, you are much more likely to have them give you their first name without having to ask for it. Once you have their first name.... USE IT! People feel important and special when they hear their name, and it makes a conversation more personable. Ask questions and then shut up.

"The best way to show customers you value them is to listen, hear them out. We were given two ears and one mouth for a reason"

Treat each call that comes into your business like gold. That's what pays the bills, and that is what buys you the lifestyle you have chosen. If you have a staff person who handles a majority of the inbound calls, you need to make sure they fully understand that it's your image on the line each and every time they pick up the receiver to say hello. The phone is our first opportunity to make a positive impression on your marketplace, and there isn't an opportunity to make another first impression.

If your business lives completely online, then these same techniques can be used to evaluate each element of your brand that exists on someone's computer and phone when they bring up your website or social media platforms. Although you may not have a brick and mortar location, your prospects still make judgments about you in 5 seconds and will decide if they are interested in spending their hard-earned money with you……or not!

The 2nd category of the 5-Second Image Challenge is the Physical Inventory and that means taking a close look at every aspect of your business. As I mentioned earlier, it may be difficult for you to look at your business objectively, and you may want to ask someone to take this journey with you.

The thought I want you to keep in the front of your mind through this entire process is this - who is my perfect customer? Do you want to cater to old school, new school, or somewhere in-between? There's plenty of both to go around, you just need to know who your perfect customer is when trying to understand the dynamics of your brand.

Physical Inventory

We are going to start with the outside of your entire business, whether it be retail us out of your home, so if you're located out of your home. If you have a retail location, drive down the street a couple of blocks and turn around. As you go through this process, it's important you write down everything you notice, and I suggest you create 2 columns.

One column will be for things that can be taken care of rather easily, like raking leaves or washing a window, and a 2nd column for things that may require a financial investment or a large amount of time, like painting the fence or getting new furniture.

Now, you want to put yourself in the mind of the consumer or your perfect customer. As you make your way closer, make a note of everything you see. Remember everything a potential customer observes about your business goes into what they are going to be willing to pay for your products and services.

"The higher the perceived value you have to your clients, the more you can charge, and the more referrals you get"

As you stand outside and observe your business, consider the following questions:

- Are there weeds on the side of the driveway that need to be taken out?
- What about any fence you may have?
- Is it in good shape, or could it use a couple of nails and a fresh coat of paint?
- What about the stripes that separate the parking spots?
- Are they freshly painted or are they faded from age?
- How does the paint look around the building?
- Does it look fresh and crisp, or does it remind you of the QuikMart next to the lake?
- Are the shrubs and bushes properly trimmed and groomed?
- Are your flower baskets overflowing with weeds and dead flowers?
- What about the lawn? Do you have a regular scheduled day each week when the mowing is done, and maintenance is performed?

Look at the sidewalk, or the walkway:

- Are there weeds growing up in the cracks, are their cigarette butts, and gum wrappers in visible sight?
- Are there dead leaves scattered all over the ground?
- Do you deadhead your flowers on a regular basis?
- What about the windows?
- Are there consistently washed, or can you see fingerprints and

dirt on them?

Having a top-quality image means that some things go unnoticed. If a window is clean, you don't even notice it, do you? But you will notice if there are prints and smudges all over it. If the grass is neatly mowed, you don't notice that it doesn't need mowing. Keep an open mind as you go through this process.

Now, we are going to walk inside your business for the first time:

- Does your entrance way invite you in?
- Do you have clear and legible signs that shows your hours of operation?
- Is it professionally done, or do you use a dry erase board?
- As you walk in, how does it make you feel? Does it give you that WOW feeling?
- Does that feeling match the image you want to build?
- What smells do you notice?
- Is it fresh and clean, or old and musty?
- What part of your business do you see first?
- Does it look clean and organized?

"When people walk into one of my businesses, I want them to feel something, an emotion that evokes a positive reaction"

Above all, make sure that the feeling you get must match with your personality, style and ultimately, your personal and professional goals. I don't pretend to be the highfalutin type, with a baby grand piano and Victorian furniture spread around.

That's just not who I am, and it's not my style. We each have our own individual style, and I like mine to be a little on the countryside of life.

We each build our business, image, or marketing programs around who we are as human beings. Before they even get a sniff of what we charge for our products and services…. They know who we are and what we can do for them. Once we have them hooked on everything else, our prices become secondary.

- How do your walls look?
- Is there dust on the pictures, or cobwebs in the corner?
- What about the lighting?
- Are all the lights working, or do you have a couple that have burned out over time?
- Are the bulbs the proper wattage?

Take notice of the carpet:

- Are there stains from spilled sodas, and pizza parties, and potato chips ground in?
- Does the color of your carpet match the feeling you want to evoke?
- What about your seating…… do you keep current with the latest styles and fabrics?
- Are your reading materials kept current, or do you still have the 1999 issue of People magazine?
- Do you have books of fine art for your customers to browse, or do you have a bin full of Comic books?

Anything you have is okay, if it fits in with the image you want for your business, and what image you want to show your customers.

"Perception is a powerful motivator."

Are your shelves and counter tops wiped down on a regular basis? Do you have candles located around your business that add a sense of quality to the air? When a customer walks into your business or home for the first time, all their senses are on high alert? Sight, sound, touch, and smell. All those senses go into how they “feel”.

Not everybody has top of the line designer leather furniture and turn of the century Victorian art pieces in their business, but we each need to make sure what we do have, is equal to the image we want to create, and the perfect customer we want to do business with.

Take the same steps with your public bathrooms, and hallways to and from. The image of your entire business is like one big apple pie, and everything we have talked about are vital ingredients in making the best apple pie recipe we can.

Do you have snacks available in case they want something to munch on? I know a several business owners that will take a fresh batch of chocolate chip cookies every single day and you can smell ‘em as soon as you get out of the car. That makes a person feel good inside. Anything you can do to make that customer enjoy themselves even just a little bit more is worth doing. If customers enjoy themselves during their time with you, they will spend more money, and will send you more referrals.

That’s it for the Physical Inventory Challenge -how did you do? You hopefully have a few pages of projects and things to do in and around the business/home over the next several weeks and months. Don’t feel overwhelmed with the amount of stuff you wrote down. It just shows you have lots of potential for future growth and improvement.

To make it a bit more manageable, you can break your list up into a weekly task list. Get your staff involved, and your family, or have a neighborhood work party, and throw everyone a BBQ complete with beverages as their payment. Have some fun with it, and get other people excited about getting involved. Life is meant to be enjoyed, whether we are playing, or working.

If your storefront is virtual, meaning that your business exists

100% online, then it is even more vital that you have everything meticulously groomed with a fine-tooth comb. You must treat your website and social media platforms as if they were a brick and mortar storefront and evaluate each element in the same way you would if you had a physical location.

Marketing Inventory

Once you are done with the Physical Inventory, it's time for the 3rd category…. The Marketing Inventory. This one, you can sit down for. You will need to grab every piece of printed literature you have such as business cards, price list, brochures, information handouts, reorder forms, coupons, contracts, direct mail pieces, newspaper ads, yellow page ads, anything you hand out, mail out, or stuff into something….and of course a good cup of coffee! Put everything in a pile in front of you and go through each piece one at a time.

"Our marketing literature is a big determining factor in what position we occupy in the mind of the consumer"

The quality of the paper it's printed on, the font selection, the quality of the ink, the color of the paper stock, the way we present it to our customers. It's all part of the apple pie. Do we just hand them a piece of paper with our prices on it, or do we package it in an elegant envelope, with gold foil lettering, finished with a gold seal? Perception, Perception, Perception.

It all depends on the industry you are in, where you want to position your business, and what lifestyle choices you have made for yourself and your family.

If you are not exactly sure how to improve on what you already have, take a look at some of your competitors literature, and at some marketing materials from other industries such as your life insurance policy, Franklin mint plate sales flyers, the welcome kit from your local Chamber of Commerce, sales flyers you get in the mail, wedding invitations you have received, the list goes on and on.

These are all things that can give you fresh ideas on how to improve your marketing literature. You can do anything you want, if you just open you mind up to new and innovative ideas from outside of the box. I challenge you to invest some time and money to create a unique look for your business that is unequalled in your market.

There are a few other very simple ways you can enhance your image and create greater value for your products and services.... Say thank you.... Any opportunity you have to say those 2 magic words should be treasured and taken advantage of. We should all never pass on a chance to make our customers feel special and appreciated. This alone can make all the difference in the world in your business this year!

"Say thank you and mean it. Say it a lot"

Send thank you notes within 24 hours of their visit or call them to say thank you for their Internet order. I can guarantee that whatever industry you are in, hardly ANY of your competitors will be taking this extra step to assure they are taking care of their prospects or customers in that fashion.

You have other occasions to touch their lives during the year also such as special cards on their birthday, anniversary, job promotion, awards they receive, Holiday cards, or for no reason whatsoever. You will be amazed how much goodwill you can create from simple gestures like this.

***"There are two kinds of service - great and bad.
The mediocre makes little or no impression on most people"***

Make it your goal to go above and beyond the call of duty when it comes to providing gold medal top-notch #1 rated customer service. This is the best way to create customers for life and keep the referral highway filled with traffic. Remember…. referrals are FREE.

The most difficult part of the wonderful world of branding is learning to understand the way the world around us works. The way perceptions are created, and judgments are made about you, and by you.

How value, and perceived value, is ultimately controlled by you, and how the entire process begins with the creative juices only you can provide. Your brainstorming can lead to incredible breakthroughs for your business, and your life without brainstorming, we wouldn't have things like ice cream cones or toilet paper.

I want to share a story about the Vice President of Marketing of a Fortune 500 company who had an innovative idea for a new product. The rest of the board had their hesitations about his idea, but he believed so firmly that he convinced them to grant him permission to proceed with the project. A few months later, when the project had completely and utterly failed, at the tune of about $3 million dollars, the VP was clearing out his office one afternoon, when the President of the company walked in.

"Where are you going?" the President asked. "I'm clearing out all my personal things and going home. I just made a huge mistake that cost your company $3 million dollars. I assumed I was fired!" he said.

"Are you crazy?" the president said, "I just invested $3 million dollars in your education."

Every idea you come up with isn't going to be a homerun, and many will probably end up being strikeouts. There is nothing worse in this world than never even swinging the bat. Risk is part of success. Those who are willing to stick their neck out each day like you do, are the true heroes of our industry.

"You cannot experience the joy of discovering new lands, if you never risk losing sight of the shore"

Perception is Everything

Brand perception is incredibly important in business, especially when it comes the prices you choose to attach to your products and services. Do you want to be perceived as expensive and exclusive, or cheap and average? Are you perceived as a newbie in the industry or an expert? Perception holds more meaning than you can imagine, especially when it comes to pricing in your business.

I once knew a businessperson who had been in his industry for over 40 years and was known for his award-winning work. He had vast numbers of international and national awards hanging on his wall, had a past client list that included Presidents and movie stars, and was one of the best there was.

Here's the flip side of that coin....his store front looked like it was painted in the 60's (which it was!), his marketing collateral was printed using outdated fonts and cheap paper, and his business cards were kept in his back pocket so they had the infamous "butt curl".

The furniture throughout his office was dated and smelled musty, which left the air void of any fragrances that evoked positive emotions.

Business had gotten so tough for him that he had been dropping his prices over time to the point that he was barely able to cover his costs. His products were delivered to his high-end clients in cheap plastic bags that he bought at the local Dollar Tree. His brand was broken.

It didn't matter how great he was at what he did, the perception was that he was not a professional and his business suffered because of that perception.

Just down the street was another business in the same industry that had just opened. The owner had decided that after a 15-year career in the advertising game she would try her hand at something new.

Her store front was warm and inviting with fresh colors and modern design elements. When you walked in there was a captivating fragrance of fresh-baked cookies, her walls were filled with modern art with designer frames, and her products were delivered in elegant branded boxes with tissue paper that matched the colors of her logo. Every detail about the customer experience was painstakingly thought about and executed on.

In comparison, her prices were triple her competition, yet she seemed to always be busy. It had nothing to do with the quality of her work but had everything to do with what her perceived value was. People gladly paid a premium price for her products, and it had nothing to do with how long she had been in the industry.

Once you have decided where you want to position and brand yourself in the price market, it will be very difficult to change, unless you decide to go through a re-brand. Remember, once a potential customer believes something, it is virtually impossible to change their mind.

"When a customer complains about price, you just haven't shown them enough value for the price you are asking"

You should be proud of your prices! "Yes, we are the most expensive, but let me tell you why………"

Your prices need to be based on what the market will bear, not on your expenses. If your prices are too low, it will scare people away. It's not that our clients won't pay our prices, but rather that we are afraid to charge what we are worth. This doesn't mean you need to raise your prices through the roof tomorrow, but you do need to be acutely aware of your current price position in the market and have a well-defined course of action on where you want to be in the future.

If you want to position yourself differently down the road, start making changes TODAY that will lead you down the road to success. Don't wait another day to make the necessary changes to assure a better tomorrow.

The key to good branding is you must be heard and must be noticed in a crowded marketplace. You want people to talk about you and be able to easily find you. Your goal is to first create awareness for yourself, then to create value.

> Regardless of what you are selling, I guarantee there is someone else out there selling it cheaper, better and faster. So why would they pay more for your product or business? The key is in your perceived value. They need to "think" they will get more from you than the guy down the street. If you don't already believe in yourself and your ability, why would anyone else?

It's like the often-told story of Picasso who was sitting outside one day and a woman passing by asked if he would do a quick sketch of her likeness. When he was done the lady asked, "How much do I owe you?

He said, "That will be $2000 please." The lady said, "For 20 minutes of your time?" He said, "No, for a lifetime of experience."

If you have something great but don't have a way of letting people know about it, you will fail.

Pricing Perception

Pricing is a very interesting part of a customer's perception. If you are known to be the lowest priced business in your market, you will never be associated with high quality or great service. If you walked onto a car dealership and saw a BMW for sale for the price of a Ford Escort, you would be leery and suspicious. Something must be wrong with it to be priced that low. The opposite is also true - If a Volkswagen were for sale for the price of a Mercedes Benz, there wouldn't be many takers.

A few years ago, I had a riding lawn mower I decided to sell, and so I took an ad out in the local paper asking $50. It had seen better days, but it still ran and would cut grass just fine. I just didn't want to be bothered with the hassle of trying to sell it. A week went by and not a single call. The second week went by, nothing. By the third week, I began to realize what was taking place, and raised the price up to $200. BAM! The calls came flooding in, and I got the asking price. Priced at $50, people thought there must be something wrong with it, and so there were no takers.

What Are You Worth?

What are you worth? More importantly... what do you want to be worth? When you work for yourself, you have both the joy and the anguish of deciding what your products and services are worth to someone else, and to figure out ways to communicate that with potential customers. If you want to be known as the low guy on the totem pole, which I hope nobody out there does, you will never be known for offering the best quality or the best service.

"We always expect to pay more for good quality, and great service"

No questions asked. When you want to go out to a nice meal complete with soft candlelight and romantic music playing, with a gourmet wine selection and hand-carved chocolate bunnies for dessert, you will pay a premium fee. We call this selling the sizzle with the steak. When you want something quick and easy without all the glitz and glamour, you will pay substantially less.

How do people perceive your business? Are you the intimate little bistro where you would expect to spend $100 on a nice meal, or are you the drive-through where $2.95 will get you the works? More importantly, where do you want to be in the future?

There will always be plenty of business at the bottom of the pile, but it comes with a very high price. The old saying, "It sure is lonely at the top," but the lunches are much better.

"Customers don't pay us for the cost of our time; they pay us for the value of our time, and the value we bring to their life"

If we show up 10 minutes late for a meeting wearing flip-flops and a T-shirt, it shows the customer we don't value ourselves very much, so why should we expect them to value us? If you want to be a Cadillac, act like a Cadillac, dress like a Cadillac, and project an image like a Cadillac.

If people like you and refer others to you- that has tremendous value. It means there is a demand for your time, which means you can charge more for your products and services. Your prices need to be based on what the market will bear and what your perceived value is, not simply on your expenses.

You cannot NOT brand your business, just like you cannot NOT communicate. If someone calls you and you answer the phone, you are branding. If someone calls and you don't answer the phone, you are still branding your business. If your business card is wrinkled and stained and is in the shape of your butt, you are communicating a message.

Positioning comes down to how others view you. Branding is the way you shake hands, the way your voice sounds on the phone, how you look, how you walk, it's as much style as it is substance. The best marketing plan costs your absolutely nothing.

When you go to the store and buy something, you aren't just buying a product you are buying a perception that the product is going to fill a need that you have.

If you want to be viewed as a professional you must dress, act, and be a professional. Don't walk into an important meeting with a 50-

cent pen and expect them to spend $5000 with you. Something as simple as a pen can paint a picture in your client's mind, either a positive image or a negative one. If you are the $99 Get-You-Everything guy, then a .50 cent pen will be more than enough, but if you have bigger fish to fry, you need to be aware of what is happening.

How do you create value for yourself? One of the key ways to create a higher perceived value is to under-promise and over-deliver every time in your business dealings. If you tell your customer their order will be done in four weeks, make sure they are ready in 3. If you quote someone $500 on a project, come in less. It's all part of giving them that positive experience that will reap rewards for your years to come.

I love a group called Mannheim Steamroller and their leader Chip Davis. Many of you may recognize the name, and if not, you would be familiar with their music if you heard it on the radio. You can walk into any music store year-round and find a big display of their music, and it's never on sale. What they do to motivate us to purchase is they will include a free CD of holiday music, or will send you a free BBQ sauce kit, or a large tin of gourmet hot chocolate.

I am one of those people who will always look for the unique and different, and their approach to branding is just that. With millions of album sales to their credit, I'm surprised more musicians haven't borrowed the technique. From personal experience, I can tell you the BBQ sauce goes great with chicken, and the hot chocolate is wonderful on those cold nights in front of the fire!

Here's a rule of thumb that I encourage you to make part of the fabric of your business. Don't discount.... Give stuff away... Let me say that again.... Don't discount. Give stuff away.

"When you discount- you penalize good clients and attract the price shoppers"

Instead of offering some sort of discount that attract clients into your business, and diminishing the perceived value of your products, give them something for free that adds value to their purchase, or brings some joy to their lives."

The fun part for you as a High-Voltage Branding wizard, you can do anything you want, just make sure it's something they can't get from any of your competitors. That way you continue to gain ownership of your hook and category each day. Obviously, whatever you do needs to make sense financial, and only you know what your restrictions and limits are.

One thing you will find as you begin to brainstorm and come up with creative marketing and branding programs is that you will have some good ideas, and some not so good ideas, and you have to be willing to try them both.

Whether you are Bic pen in your market or the Cross pen, and there is plenty of room for both, adding value to your customer's lives should be one of the most important aspects of your branding philosophy. There is always a way to add value, whether it be real or perceived.

The most difficult part of the wonderful world of Branding is in learning to understand the way the world around us works. The way perceptions are created, and judgments are made about you, and by you. How value, and perceived value, is ultimately controlled by you, and how the entire process begins with the creative juices only you can provide. Your brainstorming can lead to incredible breakthroughs for your business, and your life.

Real vs. Perceived Value

How do you create value for yourself? As mentioned in the

previous chapter, one of the keyways to create a higher perceived value is to under-promise and over deliver every time. Value is not the same as cost. Cost is what we pay to purchase something. The value of something to our customer needs to be significantly more than the selling price or they don't have an incentive to buy.

Let's say you have a product in your business that sells for $100, or should I say you want to sell for $100. Most of us can think of something in our business that sells for that price point. Through all your marketing efforts, and advertising, and promotional pieces, and positioning, and image creation, you want customers to flock to your business, whether it be physical or online, and pay $100 for let's say it's a Black Super Sonic Whatsahoosit-Plus widget. Now, whether you are successful at selling the Black Super Sonic Whatsahoosit-Plus widget is completely dependent on value or the "perceived value" it has to your client. Basically, one of three marketing phenomena is going to take place.

First, your client's perception of your widget is only $50, in which case you would have to discount by 50% in order to have a successful campaign. This is a popular technique before the holiday, or after the holidays for many of the chain stores. They motivate us with a very deep discount to lure us into the confines of their retail store, in the hopes you will purchase more than the item that is 50% off.

Groceries stores are famous for this technique. They will run an ad for $1.49 milk, or .29 Black Olives, or ears of corn 10 for a buck… and on your way to the farthest corner of the store to pick up your gallon of milk… you pass large end cap displays with 600 rolls of paper towels, or 1000 cans of pumpkin pie filling, or cherry cordial for .99 cents, and you can rest assured those items carry with them a nice profit margin.

The stores know intimately through their marketing research that for every 10 gallons of milk they sell at $1.49, they will also sell a fair number of other products as well. They make up for their discount on milk with sales from other high profit items. This technique is called using a "loss-leader" to attract customers in the door that can easily be adapted to a smaller business.

Second, the customer's perception of your widget is right at $100. Not more, not less. Right at $100. This is strategically worked to perfection by companies like Starbuck's, Apple, and Tesla. They create a demand for their products in such a way that we will gladly pay the asking price, just so we can be associated with that product. It's more about our image and making us feel special than it is what price we pay. They have made us believe that the price really isn't that important. We want to belong to the "club" so to speak.

When you go to buy a Tesla, the asking price is also the selling price… No dickering, no negotiating. If you want to drive a Tesla and belong to their "brand", this is the price. If you are a 'Buckhead", someone who gets their coffee at Starbuck's, the same dynamic is at play.

Third… You manage to create a "perceived value" in the mind of the customer some point more than $100. Maybe it's $120, maybe $150, maybe $200 or more. The greater the discrepancy between the selling price and the perceived value, the higher the level of motivation your customer will have, and the greater the level of sales you will have. This is done primarily by adding additional value to their purchase. The sky really is the limit here, and the more creative you get, the better your response will be. Remember one of the basic rules of marketing…

"Either you are different and unique, or you are out of business. Find out what everyone else is doing, then don't do it. Run as fast as you can in the other direction"

This is how you guarantee you will separate yourself from the rest of the pack.

Look at the infomercials on TV. They will spend the first 25 minutes of the show creating a value in our minds of $19.95…. And most of the time, we probably believe that's what the product is worth. Then suddenly, they sweeten the pot and say, "If you call in the next 7 minutes, we will include a second one absolutely free." You see it time and time again, so it obviously works, or they wouldn't continue doing it.

If the value in the mind of the customer is greater than the asking price, BOOM…. You have a good chance of making the sale. The bottom line in all this is simple…

"Always give your customers value that is greater than the price they pay"

That's the question of the day… How can we create a value in our products (perceived or real), that motivates people to want to do business with us? Perceived Value is strongly influenced by emotion, ego, personal image, things that are intangible and should all be considered in your marketing programs.

One thing you will find as you begin to brainstorm and come up with creative marketing programs is that you will have some good ideas, and some not so good ideas, and you have to be willing to try them both. An idea I tried a few years ago for my wedding business sounded great at the beginning but turned out to be a lot of work in the end, and I'm sure you'll see why after I tell you this story.

Back in the 1990's I had photography a business and was looking for an innovative idea that I could use to entice and motivate potential customers to book me instead of my competitors. So, I went out and purchased a professional limousine company, complete with a chauffeur and website. Originally, I was going to use it for people who signed a contract for "X" amount during the winter, but I ended up using it the entire year. My idea was this: The higher the level of investment with me, the higher the amount of time the customer was able to use the limo.

For example, if the customer purchased my "Whopper" package (much more on this in the Pricing for Profit chapter), they would get a nice limousine for 5 hours to do whatever they wanted. Well, instead of working some sort of arrangement with a local limo company, I decided to just go out and purchase the entire company.... Lock, stock and barrel!

The idea was a tremendous success. Our closing rate went through the roof, and we became the "talk of the town." Our customers absolutely loved what we did for them, but I had just purchased a business, complete with a toll-free number and yellow page ad! The calls came in at all hours from 8am Sunday morning to 11 o'clock Tuesday night for weddings, birthday parties, anniversaries, business get-togethers, sweet-16 parties. It was a real business, which meant I had to arrange coverage 24/7, for the phone and for a driver.

Many times, I ended up being the chauffeur, the mechanic, and the person who washed the limo. It did very well as a business, but it became very time-consuming and took the focus away from what the original intention was which was to provide my customers with something unique and different that would position my studio in their minds as a cut above the competition. After about 1 year, I decided to sell the company and move on to other ideas.

For the next 15 years, I longed for the days when I could hire my chauffer to take me and my fiancé out to dinner or for a drive around the lake. Finally, I decided to go out and purchase another limousine, but this time it was for selfish reasons alone. Like with so many other of my endeavors, I don't know how to think small, so eventually built the business up to the point where we were the largest wine tour service in Oregon with over 8,000 customers a year taking a tour with us. I sold the business as soon as every other limousine company started copying my techniques, but I sure had fun in the meantime!

Regardless of the outcome of your ideas, you must be willing to risk failure in order to attain the highest level of success.

"Be bold, be adventurous, and have some fun"

As you can see, creating value for yourself and your company takes on many different faces and comes in a vast plethora of colors. It's all up to you and what your goals are in life. It's very easy for us to fall into that old management trap and get caught-up in the day to day details of running our business.

We end up running of our businesses instead of designing our lives We all fall prey to it from the day-to-day stuff such answering phones, meeting with prospects and customers, ordering supplies, mowing the lawn, etc. Before we know it, our free time is gone, and there is no time for the things in life that are truly important, like family and personal hobbies.

For example, you might be working Friday nights, Sunday mornings, and holidays. You don't have time to play with your children or take a drive with your family along the lake or read that good book you've been meaning to get to or practice your putting at the golf course. The things that are most important to us start slowly slipping away and we become a slave to our business rather than its master

Whether you are the top of your market or somewhere in the middle, and there is plenty of room for both, adding value to your customer's lives should be one of the most important aspects of your branding philosophy. There is always a way to add value. Not everyone can be the Cadillac, in fact there's only 1, and not everyone wants to buy a Cadillac. Some people want to buy a Lexus, or a Tesla, or a minivan, or a Ford Escort, or a Mustang.

It's okay to borrow other ideas from within your industry, and outside of your industry. You don't need to reinvent the wheel. Just find an idea that already exists and customize it to meet your personality and style.

"Since you can't be all things to all people, find what you are good at, and make it your trademark- your personal stamp."

The day of Jack-of-all-Trades is long gone, and the age of specialization is upon us. Whatever position or niche you want to occupy in the customer's mind, everything you do should be with that in mind, and be consistent with your goals and objectives.

We have the honor and the privilege to not only sell fine products and services to our customers, but to sell ourselves as well. Believing in yourself and your abilities as a branding powerhouse can bring you rewards too great to number. The challenge of creating effective branding programs that position yourself in exactly the place you want to be, can be difficult at times, but also one of the most fulfilling and rewarding feelings you will ever have, but you have to be willing to run away from the rest of the crowd.

Separating yourself from the rest of the pack is never easy, but can take you to places never dreamed of, if you are willing to take the risk.

"Life is NOT a spectator, sport"

Personal Branding

To many people, their personal brand (PB) is what makes them successful in their chosen field. You may be one of them. Your entire business model is built on you as a person, your personality, your trust factor, your essence. If you look at some of the top brands in the world, you will notice that at the forefront of their brands is an individual- someone who encapsulates the very essence of what the company stands for. I'm going to give you a short quiz and I want you to envision the brand in your mind.

Microsoft

Amazon

Facebook

Tesla

Dallas Mavericks

When you saw the name of the business, what was the first thing that popped into your brain? Was it a logo, or was it a person? Did you see Bill Gates, Jeff Bezos, Mark Zuckerberg, Elon Musk and Mark Cuban before you thought about any logo? This is the power of PB, and your reputation and image are probably intimately tied to the brand of your business.

Self-branding can help increase your reputation as a leader, position yourself as the expert in your industry or become an influencer within your niche. You can build a personal brand that resonates with people all over the world by having an active presence in person and online and showcasing your business, talents, or skills.

It's more about creating a brand around *YOU* as a person, rather than strictly the business. In other words, PB can further your career by positioning yourself as the expert in your field, grow your social following that could lead to a better job, increase your opportunities and sell more products or services in your business. Online educators, authors, personal YouTube channels, celebrities and sports stars all have personal brands that create value for their "empires".

It doesn't happen overnight because it takes some planning and hard work to see results. In the process, you may discover that you have room for improvement after receiving feedback from others.

One way to get started is to create a personal branding statement that clearly defines your audience and what you can offer them. Place this statement in a visible place in your office, on your computer, and on your phone to remind yourself to stay true to that statement.

Credibility

People buy from people they like...plain and simple. PB gives you more credibility and is so important in this day and age when more people are looking for people and brands, they can put their trust in.

In order to get noticed, you need to put yourself out there! It's about creating a portfolio about YOU. As a result, more people will get to know you, realize the value you bring to the table, and can lead to more referrals in whatever your industry is.

New Opportunities

PB can also help you get new opportunities, marketing partnerships, and business deals that you would not otherwise hear or know about. Branding yourself instills credibility and trust in your abilities and knowledge and allows you to show your personality that differentiates you from others in your field. Aligning with your personal branding statement will help you continue and make progress with your goals.

Steps to create your personal brand:

1) Create your PB statement.
2) Define your perfect customer.
3) Plan to engage with your target audience and promote positive participation with them. (Chamber Greeters, Rotary Club, Kiwanis, networking groups, online Facebook groups, etc.)
4) Commit to sharing your personal brand through networking, speaking engagements, and social media.
5) Celebrate the small and big wins as this will keep you motivated!

How can you tell if you are being successful at your personal branding efforts?

- You get asked to speak at a conference or event.
- Someone else refers you to a potential customer or client
- A publication (online or in print) asks you to write an article or blog
- You get the sale or project
- People mention you on social media, their blog or online

Be Patient

Personal branding is time-consuming and frankly, never ends! Slacking off is never good and you must keep in tune with your industry. Take the time to delve deeper into your industry and ask the hard questions that will help you remain true to yourself and your personal/professional goals.

Be Consistent

PB requires you to be consistent in your work, beliefs, and recognize that your followers identify with you, often in more ways than one. If you change any of the above, they will not trust you or your personal brand in the future. And it is not just about making posts on social media every single day. It is also about unifying your message with the same look when it comes to personal branding. Give your audience and customers what they fell in love with in the first place.

Be Authentic

What makes you original? What are your special traits? Are you quirky about something – perhaps how you present yourself to the world? What makes you stand out? Personal branding is about celebrating your differences and requires you to be authentic as you let your true self shine.

Become a Blogger

If you are consistent in creating content, you will be amazed at how blogging can create and build an audience around you and your business. You can start out by offering to create a blog in your industry publications or build your own blog. Using blogging for your personal branding is an excellent way to build an audience around you and it allows you to create online value for your business.

Give Value to Your Audience

Give, give, give….and give some more! Whatever service or business you are in, it is important to give value to your audience and customers. That could include informative articles about specific products or services, tip of the day, or tutorial videos. Your customers could certainly buy from a company that simply runs endless ads, but by giving value to your audience, you will gain their loyalty because you taught them something of value. Give, give, give….and give some more!

Network

You must put yourself in front of the buying public and that means mingling with people at social events or conferences, joining a meet-up event, posting on social media consistently, and interacting with people as much as possible. This is what networking is all about and allows you to expand into other areas or categories that you may have never thought about. You may meet someone who can offer assistance or experience in an area that you would like to expand on in the future. You never know where networking will lead!

Be Creative

While I know it is important to be consistent with your message, you can certainly be creative when it comes to social media such as Facebook or Instagram. Showing your "personal" side may help build your credibility as a professional. You will be amazed how much it can strengthen your personal branding efforts.

Position Yourself as The Expert

What is your niche? Do you sell product online? Build your personal brand around your expertise. For example, if you are in the fitness industry, build your brand around your specialty in that arena. Write articles, help people lose weight and encourage them to share their experience with you.

Interact with Your Followers

Your personal brand cannot be built without interacting with people, especially your followers. Take time each day to respond to their messages. If someone tagged you in their post, acknowledge it and thank that person. If you wrote an article and discovered it was shared on social media, thank them for doing that. If one of your followers has a question about you or your business, take the time to answer their question. All the above will help cultivate and personalize you and your personal brand.

Developing a "Blue Ocean" Strategy

When it comes to branding your business, you have 2 choices. Have a business that offers the same products, the same services, the same everything as all your competitors. OR, you can figure out a way to develop a niche where there is very little or no competition. This is called finding some blue ocean somewhere in the world.

You may already be aware of the terms 'red ocean' and 'blue ocean,' which were coined by professors Chan Kim and Renee Mauborgne through their international best-seller book "Blue Ocean Strategy".

Basically, a market that is full of competitors is known as the red ocean because all that competition turns the ocean a blood red. If you are already a business owner in today's business world, you may have been trying to figure out what you can do to blast the competition. However, do you really want to operate in that highly competitive red ocean, or would you rather figure out a way to be a pioneer in an ever-expanding blue ocean?

The hard part is dealing with all the copycats that come out of the woodwork and take advantage of the many mistakes you have made, your ideas and strategies. In other words, they can force you back into the red ocean, especially in this high-tech Internet world we live in. What can you do when you are in blue water when it is slowly turning red? It is possible to stay in the blue water and grow a profitable business, but first let's look at the differences between the red and blue ocean:

- In a red ocean, the competition already exists whereas in a blue ocean, you can create an unchallenged market space.
- The strategy in a red ocean is to beat the competition whereas in the blue water, you make the competition irrelevant.
- The competition may have an advantage in the red ocean, but the blue ocean requires innovation and value.
- The red ocean has existing customers, but the blue ocean attracts non-customers.
- Existing demand is exploited in the red ocean whereas in the blue ocean, new demand is created.

Surviving in A Red Ocean

Entrepreneurs and business leaders are constantly creating competitive strategies in a red ocean. They go head-to-head with their competition day-in and day-out over the same consumer markets. All of them are doing the exact same thing but trying to compete on price. You will never win that battle, that I know for sure.

Let's look at fast-food chains such as McDonalds, Burger King, Arby's, Wendy's, Taco Bell. In order to survive, they have had to offer more items, install faster ordering systems, and cater to those interested in eating healthier meals. I can't remember the last time I saw a fast food chain that didn't have a "$1 Value Menu" displayed prominently on premises. The increased competition turns the water red fighting for more profit and growth, meaning the pressure to lower prices becomes immense.

Ways to Create A Blue Ocean

In a blue ocean, demand for services and business is created rather than waging war against your competition. There is plenty of opportunity for growth that is swift and profitable. Blue oceans can be created in two ways:

1) A company or business creates a brand-new industry – for example when Netflix first came out, nobody really had heard of watching a movie or a show on demand streaming on the Internet. We used to have to wait a year in order to watch "The Grinch" or "It's A Wonderful Life" on TV or watch a rerun of "Friends". Now, at the touch of a button we can watch just about every show ever created. If you have noticed, Netflix now has a RED OCEAN of competition... So, what did Netflix do a few years back? They began creating original content which kept them a step ahead of the competition. They "created" blue waters once again. Google, Apple and Disney among others have jumped into the crowded space in the last little bit of time, and as this book is written, that blue ocean is once again turning red. I'm sure someone will come up with an innovation to the industry that will make the competition irrelevant for a short period of time, then the cycle will begin all over again!
2) Create a blue ocean within a red ocean – this can occur when a company changes the limitations of an existing industry. A good example of this occurred in the saturated fitness industry with a company called Curves. Started over 25 years ago, Curves changed fitness for women by offering studio fitness workouts at a low price. The workouts last for 30 minutes and you have a coach during each session, as well as the support

members need to achieve their health and fitness goals. At the time, nobody else was offering a product or service that competed.

A few tips for finding and staying in the Blue Water:

- In order to find and stay in the blue water, you have to offer benefits that your competitors consider unnecessary or are overly unique. It might be something that contributes to a cleaner environment, offers a unique purpose, or a style that is distinctive, exclusive, rare or irreplaceable.
- Create a total solution for buyers who are purchasing a product or service. A good way to do this is to consider what goes on before, during and after a product or service has been completed.
- Create a new allure or interest in an existing product.
- Search for other segments or buyer groups for your product or service.
- Approach your business from a different perspective in time – it is not about pre-empting or predicting trends in an industry.
- Instead of focusing on customer differences, focus on prevailing unities in what customers value.
- Focus on trying to increase the size of your industry or business by attracting people who have never purchased anything in that industry before.
- Create a high value at a low cost – a good example of this is Southwest Airlines and JetBlue who appealed to people who were used to driving to their destinations, rather than flying. In other words, they made flying affordable. Strip away any unnecessary costs – anything that doesn't contribute or create value gets reduced or eliminated. Plus, it is an efficient way to run a business regardless of what color ocean you are in.

As you can see, the concept of a red and blue ocean is much easier to understand if you look at real-world examples that exist today of how businesses have branded themselves, then rebranded themselves.

Most industries are operating in a red ocean with defined competitors, with specific ways to run their business in a defined market. It is best described as shark-infested water where all the sharks are fighting for the same prey.

You must take some time to evaluate whether you need to rethink your business strategies and branding to create a blue ocean for your products and services. This is fun and challenging at the same time!

If you are spending all your time fighting for a piece of limited sales, then you are in a red ocean and you need to stop, right now! You are probably constantly competing with your competitors just to increase your market share as your business becomes more competitive and aggressive with more and more competitors coming in. Profits are likely to diminish as well, and eventually you will go out of business.

When companies compete for the same customers with the same products, same features, same benefits, the result is a pricing war and you will ALWAYS end up a loser in the scenario.

Just remember that once you are successful in the blue water, other companies will be attracted to you and quickly change your blue water space to red. When this occur, and bet your bottom dollar that it will, you must differentiate yourself. Saying that you are 'the original' only works for so long before it doesn't matter anymore. You may be forced to customize your product more or offer other services to keep yourself in the blue water, but it will be totally worth it.

Delivering a "6-Star Experience"

As the digital revolution continues to take root in our cultures, so too has the decrease in the importance of having actual humans at the front lines of a business. The Internet has taken away much of the human interaction that just a few short years ago was vitally important to business survival.

Getting gas, shopping for groceries, buying a movie ticket, getting a hot dog at a baseball game, or simply stopping at the bank to make a deposit. In my life, these are all touch points when I have the opportunity for conversation with a frontline employee during my purchase.

If I'm not greeted with at least a short and friendly *"Hello, how are you today"*, or a brief moment of eye contact, I have no problem saying *"Hello, don't forget to greet your customers"* or *"Don't forget to smile at your customers"!* It's not that I expect to have a real conversation but do expect to at least be shown a little consideration since I'm the one paying their wage!

It drives my wife and kids crazy when I do it, but it's something I feel strongly about. To most retail-type businesses, they must depend on having those frontline folks represent their brand at the highest levels, but for some unknown reason that skill has not been given the importance that it once had. It is becoming a dying art.

If you are even a little like me, you feel the same way. We expect to have a basic level of customer service when we have some sort of interaction with a business. Get it right and they continue to get our support. Blow it and we will be happy to tell our friends and family about our bad experience.

When you hear about the accolades of the best hotels and restaurants around the world, you typically hear about the "5-Star" ratings that they have. To them, and to the customers they serve, that means they are the absolute best at what they do. There's no better number than to be given 5 stars.

I think there needs to be a new level of customer service, a new scale on how our customers judge us by. I suggest we add one more star to the scale for our businesses.

Here's an example…Right now where you are sitting, I want you to reach your arms and hands as far towards the heavens as you can. Reach, reach, reach! Have you reached as far as you can? Now, I want you to reach a little bit further.

I bet you found a little more umph inside of you to reach just a bit more, didn't you? Why is that? You reached as far as you could the first time, but then you reached a little farther when asked.

"What does it hurt for us to give just a little bit more when it comes to providing impeccable customer service to our customer"

I recently had my car into the body shop to repair a small dent in the front fender. When I dropped the car of along with the keys, I inadvertently forgot to take off the master key to my office. By the time I figured this out, it was the end of the day and I couldn't leave the building unlocked to go back to the body shop to get my master key.

My solution was to have a taxi go to the shop to pick up the key, then bring it to me. When I called the body shop to let them know about the plan, they GM said he would take care of making the arrangements.

About 20 minutes later the GM himself walked into my office with the key! He drove all the way across town to fix a problem that I created, not him.

That level of service was not asked for nor expected, but it made me a customer for life with the company! Something not expected can often bring the biggest results. What can you do in your business that shows your customers that you care "just a little bit" more?

Back in the 70's there was a band called Dr. Hook, and they

cranked out some of the best love songs that this world has ever seen. One of their song's muses "when you think I've loved you all I can, I'm gonna love you a little bit more".

Having a 6-Star mentality will not only revolutionize the way your business operates but will also give you a competitive edge in the market.

What does it hurt to give just a little extra?

How to Build A Cult Brand

Water. It's everywhere and it's free.

This is a product that has always amazed me…something that we have access to for FREE, yet we gladly will pay good money for the convenience of not having to get it from our tap at home, or because we simply want to belong to the "brand".

In lakes, in the mountains, in our schools, in the showers, in our sinks. Remind me again WHY there are so many H2O brands on the shelves today when it's something we can get for free in most places?

We will spend anywhere between $1 and $10 on a single bottle of water not just to get hydrated, but to belong to a brand, or cult if you will. People that walk around with a bottle of Perrier don't do so because they are thirsty, they do it because they belong to a tribe, a group of like-minded people from all around the world that have bought into the Perrier brand. Dasani, Aquafina, Evian and more all have created cult-like followings for their brands.

We purchase over 50,000,000,000 (billion with a B!) bottles of water each year in the US alone. Worldwide that number is more than 200,000,000,000 bottles a year.

I have a secret to tell you that I'm sure most people already know, but we won't admit it to ourselves. In its purest form, water is water. There is no such thing as a "better quality" water. Assuming that it is void of any minerals or impurities and has been filtered properly, water is water. Now that we have that worked out, let's move on.

Two bottles. The same H2O inside. Two diametrically opposite markets. One is the low-end where that small bottle of water goes for pennies. The other is the high-end landscape where it goes for as much as ten bucks apiece (remember that water very similar to this is available from your sink or garden house in your back yard!). One is $1 and the other is $10. How do you pull something like that off?

Obviously through high-voltage branding where you'll first identify the "discontent" point in the high-end market; for example, "spotting a trend" (after creating a buzz!) where your targeted demographic is uncertain about what type of a glass container would be the only acceptable way to store water in its pure state. Or, perhaps, it's the source of the water that triggers the right emotion? Maybe the deep, underground reservoir containing prehistoric water would be far more marketable than just another ground-level spring or river regardless of how pure, pristine, and intact it may be in reality?

Remember, they don't know it until we tell them. They are always simply open to suggestions –.

Today's consumerism leaves no one immune to a well-targeted and well-crafted message. And that's the spot we are hitting with our prehistoric, deep underground reservoir from which we are pumping the water in its purest possible state and then store it in the high-quality glass bottles crafted in one of the world's most exclusive glass factories famous for casting glass for kings and queens.

Such an operation sounds quite expensive, doesn't it? Well, not necessarily.

Terms "deep" and "underground" are, of course, relative. Therefore, we will simply avoid mentioning the fact that we are extracting water from the five-foot deep basin.

Is it underground? Yes. Is it deep? Sure. There is no way to say how deep that goes just by looking at images and videos that are online.

If we craft a compelling story and message, people will have an emotional reaction to it. It's a basic human behavior. We want to believe. And once people are indoctrinated into our story, they will ruthlessly defend our brand at all costs.

It's not just a bottle of water. It's a statement. An ID card that our friends immediately recognize. A single, swift look and people know that we belong. It doesn't matter that we paid 1000% over the real market value, bought access. We bought a privilege.

Need I remind you that this is for something that most people in the world can get for free, with a little effort! These brands have created a sense of tribalism for their products, and with it has come tremendous profits.

"Your goal should be to create the same type of zest and zeal for your brand so that people will proclaim your name from the highest mountain top"

A cult following for your products and services. Do this, and the rest is a piece of cake! Nike, Apple, Harley Davidson, Gucci......need I say more?

Is My Brand Broke?

The question that I hope is now floating around in that big wonderful brain of yours is this...could my brand use an update? Do I need to consider a complete overhaul to my brand? Is my brand broke?

For many of you, these types of thoughts have never entered your mind before and I encourage you to sit down with that proverbial good cup of coffee and really give this topic some serious thought.

Maybe you are burned out and feel like throwing in the towel. Maybe you feel deep down that you are not meant for the entrepreneurial game. If it was easy, everyone would be jumping in the game with both feet.... but it's not. It's meant for a small handful of very special individuals who have visions for a better world, a passion to makes lives more fulfilling. *YOU* are one of the chosen few!

Whether you are a conglomerate with 1000's of employees or have an enterprise with 1 employee (you!), keeping the edge of your business sword sharp is one of the most important responsibilities you have. As time goes by, our edge can become dulled because of a variety of reasons; apathy, burnout, thinking you are too busy, business growth, or plain ole laziness.

That's ok, there's no better time than right now to put aside all your excuses and to dedicate some precious bandwidth to this topic. This book has detailed some of the steps you can take in order to answer these questions and has hopefully given you the motivation to take the branding bull by the horns.

Regardless of what your answers are, this can be one of the most exciting times in the history of your business. If you are still contemplating jumping into the entrepreneurial game, this is your opportunity to put some muscle behind your brand before it's event launch to the world. It's never easy to take the road less travelled, and to go above and beyond to make sure that you are keeping the edge of your sword sharp.

This book, in case you haven't figured it out yet, is about helping you keep your edge sharp. It's very easy to get caught up in the "cutting down of trees" that we forget to continue to sharpen our axe so that the business forest is easier to navigate.

"To get the most out of life, we must continue to be students"

It's not about just setting goals for your business. Sharpening your focus means digging deeper to gain a clearer understanding of what you really want out of life, what your true priorities are, and how to go about reaching those goals. Whatever your business brand looks like, remember to stay true to yourself and your dreams.

As I have written in other books, finding the perfect work/life balance is something we all need to focus on every day. Life is short, life is precious, and life is sometimes fleeting.

We need to make sure that we are aware of those special "moments" that present themselves to us and take advantage of opportunities to tell the people who mean the most that we love them!

Yes, your business and your job are important aspects of your life, because you need the income, they bring so you can buy the perfect lifestyle for you and your family.

But, when your time on this earth is over, all that will be remembered is the difference you made to those that meant the most to you.

Chapter 4

Blue Ocean Marketing

So, what does the word marketing mean to you? Simply defined, it means letting potential customers know who you are, what you do, and why they should spend their hard-earned money with you instead of the guy down the street or across the country. As we discussed in the chapter on High Voltage Branding, you need to find, or create, a "blue ocean" that separates you from the rest of the pack.

While the concept is a simple one, many businesspeople today put little effort into achieving these goals. They open theirs actual or virtual doors in the morning and wait for customers to come storming in. Speaking for myself, I prefer to have control over my business, and I believe you do too.

To succeed in any industry, you'll need more than a passion for what it is you do. You must have an understanding on the laws of business and a plan that is second to none. It also demands initiative, self-discipline, and a healthy dose of mental energy drawn from the depths of your creative being. Small business owners have gigantic challenges to face each and every day, whether it be the increasing costs of doing business, more competition for consumer dollars, or the need to find the energy to keep your nose to the grindstone when things get tough.

The main reason that I'm self-employed is so that I can have the ultimate say in the ways I spend my time each day, whether that be working on playing. The better your business plan, the more time off you must do the things in life that are most important to you.

We sometimes forget that running a successful enterprise requires a lot more than the day-to-day routine of running your business; it demands vision as well- the stuff from which dreams are made. It's almost mystical as it drives us each day to get up and do a better job than we did the day before. It's what *WE* have that other lack.

Whether you live in a thriving metropolis or a small town, having a well-defined marketing plan is vital to your professional success. Did you know that every ten seconds in this country there is a business that folds up its tent and goes home? That's an amazing statistic to me! If five years, 4 out of 5 businesses will not be around. And guess what most of those businesses don't have? You got it, a marketing plan!

Entrepreneurs are faced with more and more challenges and obstacles every day. There are times you just want to beat your head against the wall and chick it all in. That's because we allow our business to control us instead of us being in control.

Whether you realize it or not, you already have a marketing plan, intentional or not. It has been said that the sales process ends when the customers gives you their credit card or check. Well, everything that happens up to that point determines how large that check will be. That's where the marketing comes in. The better job you do, the bigger that invoice will be. It's not rocket science, but the lack of a well-planned strategy is one of the biggest reasons why businesses fail. The best product doesn't always win the race, the best marketer does!

You are better off being a top-notch marketing and being "just good enough" at your chosen craft than the reverse. My money will always be on the marketer every time. In business today, people buy because they want to feel good about themselves. They need to be convinced that we offer something special that will add value to their lives.

What Is Power Marketing?

Power Marketing is the opposite of passive marketing. It demands your personal proactive involvement and is very systematic. If you want to be a successful Power Marketer, you must be willing to roll up your sleeves, jump in the trenches, and get a little dirty! Sounds like fun, doesn't it? It really can be if you understand the philosophy behind it and can see the benefits you will reap over the long haul.

I once knew a man who had a very successful pet product manufacturing company, and it seemed no matter what pet store I went in to, his products were on the shelf. The packaging was professional looking and colorful, the price was fair, and it was something every pet owner used. What better combination! My opinion of the products was high, and I figured his warehouse was full of brand new, state-of-the-art machines, high-tech equipment, the employees dressed in freshly pressed uniforms, and the offices lined with expensive oak furniture.

I remember walking into his building for the first time and feeling my jaw drop to the floor. The building was the size of a large garage, there were only 3 employees (nearly all the work was contracted out) and the "executive office" was a remodeled bathroom with little room to sit. There were file cabinets everywhere, a small coffee table, and two chairs. It was very clean and organized, but *SMALL!*

I couldn't believe that such a "big" company was operating out of such a small area. When I asked the owner how he had made his company so successful though he was working with so little, his answer was short and to the point- *"Marketing, marketing, marketing!"* Although he didn't believe in excessive spending, he spared no expense when it came to presenting a professional image to his customers. Everything from the way his secretary answered the phone, to his elegant letterhead, to the way he packaged and presented his products was top-notch! He settled for nothing less but the best, and nothing was left to chance.

I remember him telling me that his image and marketing were the most powerful ways of communicating with the world, and the only thing that mattered was what the customer thought. His marketing plans were written out a year in advance, and he could show you the results from each idea he ever tried- good or bad. If something didn't work, he would either rework it and try again or move on to the next idea until he got it right!

The last time I talked with him, his annual sales were over $10,000,000. There is something to this thing they call marketing.

The Power Marketing Self-Test

Before you dive in with both feet, you need to take inventory of your current marketing efforts. So, let's begin with a quick Power Marketing Self-Test. Don't worry, there are no right or wrong answers to this test, it's just information about your business- and the more you have, the better prepared you will be when it comes to planning and executing a Power Marketing campaign.

Now, you may not have answers to all the questions in the following test. Don't worry. Simply providing any answers you will help lay the foundation for a new way of thinking. Creating a marketing plan is like building a house: A good contractor would never build a house on unstable ground or without pouring the concrete first.

So, grab a good cup of coffee and a pen and notepad. Turn off your devices, put some relaxing music on, then sit back and close your eyes for a few seconds before we begin.

All right, here we go....

1- What does your current marketing efforts consist of (i.e., postcards, Facebook/Google ads, phone books, website, referral programs, TV, radio, etc.)
2- Do you have a way of tracking the results of your current programs? What is it?
3- Do you consistently develop a list of goals before you begin a new campaign? How do you do it? How do you measure their effectiveness?
4- What have you tried in the past that didn't attain the desired results? Why?
5- What programs in the past exceeded your desired expectations? Why?
6- Do you have a plan for your upcoming marketing programs? What are they?
7- Have you identified the goals and objectives for those programs? What are they?
8- What types of marketing are your competitors using that seems to be successful? Why?
9- Do you have a budget set each month for marketing? How much is it?
10- What makes customers come to your business instead of to your competitors?
11- What makes customers go to your competitors instead?
12- As a consumer, what do you look for from a business you purchase from?
13- What are your three biggest strengths as a business owner?

14- What are your three biggest weaknesses as a business owner?

15- Do you set aside time each day to work on the essence of your business and develop new ways to improve? If not, what time of day would work best for you if you started tomorrow?

Well, how did you do? Did you have a pretty good idea of how to answer each question or did a few of them give you pause for thought? Remember, there are no right or wrong answers, only information. I challenge you to ask yourself not only these questions, but to come up with some of your own about your business and your effectiveness as a marketer.

A top-notch Power Marketer is constantly reviewing, analyzing, and adjusting their techniques to achieve their maximum potential and to get the most out of their employees and themselves. Only YOU have the ultimate responsibility; if you don't do it, nobody else will.

Whether you have been in your industry for many years or are new to the game, you probably realize that it takes guts and determination to own and operate a business. Simple, it's not. It requires a very special person who is willing to take risks, commit themselves to a cause, and to fight the daily battles in order to do whatever it takes.

If I were to list all the issues that contribute to business failure, it would fill this entire book! Of course, you can find hundreds of books on thousands of subjects pertaining to business at your local library or on the Internet. Many offer good information, many do not. I know of only one absolute truth when it comes to operating a business: there is not another business exactly like yours anywhere else in the world, and only you can decide what information is beneficial, and what isn't.

DEVELOPING YOUR MARKETING STRATEGY

Before you can develop a marketing plan, you must know what

it is you want out of life. We have already dealt with that in Chapter 1. Striking a balance between bandwidth you devote to your business and the time you take for yourself is one of the hardest skills to develop. You only have so much bandwidth to share around!

Taking It All in Stride

To achieve that balance, you need to take your job seriously but yourself lightly! It's called having a sense of humor. And having a sense of humor is not something you are born with, it's a set of developed skills that allows us to keep flexible in the face of stress and change- and it really has nothing to do with telling jokes.

Do you feel you have a good sense of humor? There are people in this world who go through life with a case of terminal professionalism. You know the type:

"If I'm going to be successful, I must be hard-driving, hardheaded, and serious. I don't have time to laugh and play around. Leave me alone- I'm having a really good bad day!"

Those are the kinds of people who end up with a nervous breakdown, end up dead, or worse yet end up as old, bitter, cantankerous competitors of yours! We need to enjoy the simple things in life…a newborn baby, a sunny day, a home run in the bottom of the ninth, a great cup of coffee!

Having a sense of humor won't solve the world's problems, but it sure makes it easier to get through the tough patches that life throws at us now and then. Such an outlook has the magical ability to sustain life. When people are on their deathbeds, they don't say they wished they owned more toys and had more money. They say things like, *"I wish I could have worked less and played more."*

Part of the reason we find it difficult to keep it light sometimes is the world we live it is full of stress. That part will never change, but we can change ourselves.

"Good marketing is not an expense, it's an investment"

Knowing Yourself and Your Priorities

Being successful has nothing to do with the amount of money in your bank account, it's about perspective. Our thoughts can keep up healthy or make us ill. It's all up to us. Success is a constantly evolving journey, not merely a destination. You set your sights on the future to map out your goals in your life, just as you do for your business with a good marketing plan.

After all, we drive with our focus in the distance, not on the highway as it passes beneath us. Remember Alice In Wonderland? When Alice was walking through Wonderland, she came to a fork in the road and met the Cheshire cat. She asked, "which road do I take?" and the Cheshire cat said, "well, where do you want to go?" Alice responded, "I don't know," and the Cheshire cat said, "then any road will get you there."

Knowing Your Customers and Their Priorities

When I was in the seventh grade, I had a business that I ran out of my garage. If you needed a bicycle chain or seat or tire, chances were I had it! If I didn't, I would trade with the guy down the street to get one. At the time I didn't understand any of the dynamics of marketing, but I sure seemed to have a lot of kids coming over!

Saturday mornings were the best; all the neighborhood kids would ride their bikes up and down the street and would stop in to see what the "hot special" was for the day. The best deal I ever made was trading a set of blue handle grips for a dollar and a 45-record (if you are younger than 40, you may not understand this reference!). I can remember playing that record until the grooves wore out!

I used to take bicycle chains and horns to school to show my friends and classmates. Mondays were always good because a lot of kids received their allowance over the weekend. Sometimes I would get a special order for a banana seat or a sissy bar and would have to trade with someone else to be able to fill the order. In junior high there were lots of guys who had so-called bike businesses, so I usually fond the requested item.

There definitely wasn't much money to be made, but looking back, I learned an important marketing principal: In order to be successful with any business, you need to understand your potential customers and then develop a strategic plan that attracts them to you. This is probably the most basic definition for the word marketing.

In the real world of business, things are a bit more difficult than when we were kids, but the rules are the same. The self-test you took earlier likely resulted in some self-discovery. Having an intimate understanding of what make you tick is not only important to your business, but your life. Knowing your strengths and weaknesses as well as what challenges and excites you, will help you to be the best you can be.

Recharge Your Personal Batteries

This is where good old quiet time comes in handy, because we all get into the 9-to-5 mentality and can become mere observers of our businesses. This outlook taxes your energy level and it doesn't allow you to focus on the real issue, which is how to make your enterprise more profitable. Nor does it free your mind to allow the expansive thinking that separates "good" from "great."

Let's compare your business to a care with a full tank of gas. At the beginning of your trip you feel pretty good driving down the road and looking at all the sites. You're excited and enthused about your journey and not too concerned with what lies down the road. As the miles go by, the needle starts to drop on your fuel gauge, and you start thinking about filling up. But the next gas station isn't for another hundred miles, so you continue driving.

If you don't get gas soon, you will end up stranded on the side of the road! Now, would you ever let your gas tank get so low that you run the risk of running it dry in the middle of nowhere? Likely not. So why would you allow your business to run for long periods of time without adding fuel to the tank?

The fuel for your business comes in the form of creative juices and mental energy. No one has as much desire to make it succeed like you do. The challenge is in figuring out a way to look at your business from an outsider's point of view. What we would like people to think of us, and what they think of us, are often vastly different. We may have the best intentions, but for whatever reasons the message doesn't come across the way we intended. We all probably have a few stories to tell.

I have a couple of friends who had been in business for over twenty years. They had become weary after that many years of keeping their noses to the grindstone through tough times and decided to close their location. After a while, they realized that working for someone else was not their cup of team, and they reopened their business.

But before they did, they had plenty of opportunity to research new and different ways of marketing, selling, branding, and just about everything related to being productive. This began to become quite enjoyable for them, and before long they had developed a head of steam that has allowed them to totally and completely reinvent the way they operate.

What a joy it has been to watch as their new vision has grown from the bottom up all over again, and as they have discovered new and exciting ways of doing things. It's almost like they are going into business for the very first time, and it's because they allowed themselves the creative freedom to brainstorm for a breakthrough!

Is this something that sounds intriguing to you? Do you have the desire to reinvent and replenish your creative juices? Brainstorming will give you the opportunity!

Be Objective in Analyzing Your Business

The most valuable asset you can have as a Power Marketer is an objective perspective. In a sense, you need to put your entire business on a table in front of you, then stand on a chair and look down upon it. Here is a simple test you can take to help identify some objective details about your business. Grab a pen and paper (and of course that good cup of coffee!) and grade yourself on a scale of 1 to 10 (10 being perfect).

1- I am totally satisfied with my staff and feel they are doing the best they can do.

2- I feel my staff is happy and content with their jobs.

3- I have a good understanding of my customer base.

4- I am satisfied with my current suppliers and know I am getting the best possible service, quality and price.

5- I believe my store front, website, and other marketing collateral are the best they can be.

6- I am satisfied with my current level of sales and profit.

7- I have a thorough understanding of my competition and know their strengths and weaknesses.

8- I feel the products and services I offer are complete, my prices fair, and my profit margins acceptable.

9- I am aware of my strengths and weaknesses are and can list them on paper.

10- I am confident that my ordering procedures and inventory levels are under control.

Now, let's see how you did. Add up the ten individual scores to see how you stack up.

90 to 100- Great job! You obviously are in touch with the pulse of your business.

80 to 89- You have a pretty good understanding of your business but realize there is room for improvement.

70 to 79- Things are becoming overwhelming to you, and you are searching for answers.

60 to 69- Your business is getting out of control and you are probably considering joining a monastery.

59 and below- You are wondering why in the world you got into this industry in the first place!

There are no pass or fail marks, only a better understanding of your business. We need to have a starting point, and now you know where yours is. If you scored lower than you had hoped, don't get discouraged. You just have more opportunities for growth!

Making Progress

Now that you have a fair idea of your business's strengths and weaknesses, it's time to look at some of the areas in which your business can be improved, no matter your score on the previous quiz.

Understanding Your Customers

We all know that our customers are, without a doubt, our most important assets. Whether you are just getting started and have a small customer base or have worked to develop one that is extremely large, it is vital that you understand everything you can about them. The value of this information will be obvious when you sit down to plan your first Power Marketing campaign.

There is a small, owner-operated coffee shop that is in a tiny town and enjoys a rather lucrative business, offering a wide variety of coffees, fresh bakery items, and a pleasant atmosphere. For many years it has been the cool place to go and hang out. It is constantly packed with patrons. There must be at least 5 or more other coffee shops within a 3-mile radius, but this lady is the best!

One day, I asked the owner what it was that lured the customers into her establishment. She said, *"I bet I can tell you the first name and favorite drink of 99% of my customers. I want each person to feel they are my most important one. Everything I do is with them in mind."*

Isn't that a wonderful message? No wonder people come from miles around to sit and visit. She makes them feel like gold! Unfortunately, not everyone has the pizazz and memory this woman has, but I bet each of us could do a better job of taking care of and listening to our valued customers.

Measuring the Competition

Throughout history, wars have been won and lost by many nations and many types of people. Some wars were fought because of differences in religious beliefs; others fought over territory disputes; and still other because of the overinflated egos of their leaders. Regardless of the reasons why people fight wars, it's a given that the winner was aware of the opponent's strengths and weaknesses and was able to adapt their battle plan in order to effectively compete.

One of the biggest fears of any entrepreneur is the fear of competition, and it doesn't matter what you do it's everywhere! Competition is vital to your success, whether you realize it or not. It requires you to constantly adjust, analyze, and adapt your own business plan to a changing market. Those who react the most effectively are the ones who end up on top, while those who don't react at all end up in a different industry!

On the flip side, we are all charged with the responsibility to both introduce new consumers to and educate them about our respective niches. In this respect, you are on the same team as every one of your competitors. But that's where the friendly competition ends. Beyond that, the consumer is the battlefield, and he name of the game is survival of the fittest. You are in business to generate profits and provide for your lifestyle choices, just like your competitors.

If I asked you to list three strengths and weaknesses of your biggest competitors, would you be able to? Most of us are acutely aware of our own strengths but won't admit any glaring weaknesses. That's just human nature. In business, however, you must be able to identify the good and bad in our own enterprise, and in others' as well.

Once of the easiest ways to learn about your competition is give them a call or have a meeting with them. Just sit down and chat with them about their challenges, their struggles, their vision. Be willing to share yours as well. There's no rule that says you can't get along with and be friendly with your competitors! Remember that we all are on the same team and it's important to help each other. You don't' have to give away any trade secrets, but you may find that you can help each other out in many ways.

The goal in marketing is not to have your competitors fail, but rather to increase your chances of succeeding. If you ask most people, they will tell you marketing is a battle of products and services. In the long run, they figure, the best product will win. *NOT TRUE!* The only things that exist in the world of marketing are perceptions in the mind of customers. Perception is reality. Everything else is illusion. What the customer perceives as fact is fact.

Identifying Your Hook

What makes your business stand out from the crowd and gives the customer a reason to come to you instead of the guy across town? What is it about you that is so compelling that people can't help but to want to do business with you? Do you know what it is? In the world of marketing, we refer to this message that we send to potential customers as a "hook," and it is probably one of the most important assets you have. Great empires have been built on great messages! If you don't know what yours is, that's another assignment for you.

It's important to mention that not everyone can have the same strengths and be best in all categories, but to maximize your position in the market, you should be tops in at least one. Which one? Well, that's up to you to figure out and decide.

"What is it that you do better than anyone else"

Well, to many companies, they have tied this answer up into a little package we call a slogan. Here's a little exercise that will show you the incredible power of a good and simple slogan. See if you can identify the companies behind each one.

SLOGANS

1- Just Do It

2- We Try Harder

3- Nothing Runs Like A Deer

4- From Sharp Minds Come Sharp Products

5- You're in Good Hands

6- Have It Your Way

7- We Care About the Shape You Are In

8- Fresh, Hot Pizza, Delivered In 30 Minutes or Less

COMPANIES

A- Wonderbra

B- Avis

C- Sharp Electronics

D- John Deere

E- Domino's Pizza

F- Allstate Insurance

G- Nike

H- Burger King

ANSWERS- 1-G, 2-B, 3-D, 4-C, 5-F, 6-H, 7-A, 8-E

Do you have a slogan, or tagline, for your business? Can you summarize your marketing message and what position you occupy in one sentence? Creating an effective marketing slogan will require some thinking on your part. It doesn't have to be complicated, but it should communicate who you are and what you want the market to know about you. The same is true of your logo. It can be something as simple as your font selection, or something with extensive graphics and colors. But whatever it is, it should appeal to the specific perfect customer you want to attract.

Make sure you are consistent with everything you do, and make an investment in your business cards, your stationary, your signage, a great website or social media platform- anything that projects who you are. Sometimes you need to spend a little money in order to make a great first impression.

While successful people may not be the very best at what they do, they use top-notch marketing to position themselves in the mind of their perfect customer better than the next business. When you go to a grocery store, do you always purchase the best product, or do you choose the one that is most cleverly marketed and has the best packaging?

Establish A Personal Connection

When it comes right down to it, the customer is attractive by your perspective, personality, sense of humor, etc... The biggest hook you can offer your customers is yourself! If you can establish a personal connection with the customers, price becomes secondary, because they are investing in you.

Following this logic, people who recognize they don't have the personality of a salesperson or a marketer will be well served to hire someone who does. Without the ability to sell yourself or sell your business, failure is not far behind. Long gone are the days when you could hang out a shingle and people would flock to you simply because you were good. In today's fiercely competitive world, only the strong will survive.

Stand Out from The Crowd

An important factor in determining what it is you do better than anyone else is to make sure someone else doesn't already make that claim.

"One of the basic rules of marketing is it's better to be first in your own category than to be second in someone else's"

You need to find an area that nobody has taken as their own, and then build on it. I once knew a business owner who had the "me too" syndrome. He always waited to see what everyone else was doing then would do the same thing. Big mistake! Over time, customers became aware he was always copying other people's ideas, and he continued to lose business until he had no choice but to get out of the industry. If he would have focused on his uniqueness, he would still be around today.

I'm going to ask you some questions about category ownership, and I want you to think of the answers:

- What is the top cell phone company? Who is 2nd?
- Who is the top rental car company? Who is 2nd?
- What is the top selling facial tissue? Who is 2nd?
- Who sells the most books online? Who's 2nd?
- Who is the #1 manufacturer of blue jeans? Who's 2nd?

While you may instantly know in your mind who is first in each category, I bet you had to stop and think about the names of runners-up.

Are you starting to get the idea? Nobody cares about or even remembers the 2nd place finisher!

Establishing Program Goals and Objectives

John Wooden, the great coach for the ULCA Bruins back in their glory days, used to sit down before each season and write down a list of goals for himself, then for each player, then for the team. Periodically during the season, he would pull them out and reread them. No other coach in the history of college basketball has had as much success as Coach Wooden, and it wasn't by chance! His ability to set goals, maximize his resources, adjust his methodology as the season progressed, and follow through until the end, produced championship after championship, year after year.

Athletics teaches us a lot about setting goals and working towards them with diligence. Your business requires the same level of commitment in order to achieve your objectives. In marketing, your goals should be based on three considerations:

1. Are the goals realistic and attainable?
2. Does the program help you achieve your ultimate goals and objectives?
3. Will the results be measurable and trackable?

If you can answer yes to all three questions, then your program has the potential to be successful. It may be worth investigating further.

POSITIONING FOR PROFIT

Do you ever find yourself saying, "It seems there are far too many ways to market and position my business? How can I know what's best?" The list below should give you some idea of the variety.

What Is Positioning?

What does the word positioning mean to you? To me it's a very simple concept: it means putting yourself in front of the exact customer you want, with precisely the message you want to communicate, at just the right time. The best part is that you can decide all these things on your own!

Revitalizing and re-energizing your marketing plan- or as I like to call it, your battle plan- is not an easy task. We began the brainstorming process with the Power Marketing Self-Test. We also talked about being able to identify what it is about your business that is unique and special, and what it is that separates you from the rest of the pack.

Either you are unique and different, or you are out of business. Having a me-too approach will not get you very far down the road to being a successful Power Marketer. The old saying- The guy at the top of the mountain didn't fall there," holds true.

There is nothing wrong with making a profit; without it, you have no business. You shouldn't feel guilty about getting paid well for what you do; it allows you to support your family, pay employees, and keep the doors open for the next time your customer comes in to do business with you.

Finding Your Niche

Before you can decide on the exact position you want to occupy in your market, you must know what you want out of life. In Chapter 1, we talked about setting personal and professional goals, and how important it is to achieve the proper balance. Now, if you are the type of person who needs to work seven days a week, from sunup to sundown, then your goals might be altogether different from those of someone like me. What is it that you need in your life to make you feel fulfilled, complete, and satisfied?

Whether it's time with your family, time at the office, or time to work on your cribbage skills, you need to have a firm grasp on what your priorities are, and therefore it will be much easier to figure out what niche you want to occupy.

THE TEN CATEGORIES OF MARKETING

If I were to get a "blue widget" something that we all sold in common and spread them out on the floor, then asked a customer to select the best, I imagine they would have a difficult time making a decision. The fact is many would look alike with the same features, same benefits, same everything. Unless you have some sort of innovative feature that brings a hidden benefit, most of the widgets would look and feel the same to a prospective customer. If that's the case, the result is a pricing war and you lose that battle every time.

Your overall goal is to somehow create extra value for yourself, your products and services so you can charge more, make more, and have more time off! Am I right? There are literally hundreds of things you can do to promote your business, but I have broken it down to 10 Categories of Power Marketing.

1-Literature

This category contains your business cards, price lists, flyers, postcards, direct mail pieces, statements, letterhead, box stuffers, brochures- and anything else that has your name and logo printed on it.

When a potential customer first lays eyes on or touches your business card, they will immediately form an opinion regarding what they feel you are worth. How does it look? How does it make you feel? What would you think if someone were to hand your business card to you? Do you use paper stock you find in the clearance bin at the local office supply store, or do you use high-quality designer stock? Remember, everything that the customer sees, touches, smells, observes, or feels goes into determining what they are willing to pay for your products and services. It's okay to use the half-priced discontinued stock if you're not aiming for an upscale reputation.

I had a gentleman approach me several years ago after a keynote speech I had given with a stack of his marketing collateral and his business card. He was struggling to stay afloat and was looking for some input and direction. I recognized his name as someone in the industry who was extremely well respected and had been around for quite some time. When he handed me the stack of papers, I knew immediately what his problem was. His business card was printed on thin paper stock with faded black ink (he printed them himself), and his price list was photocopied in his office complete with black streaks running down the middle of the page. My first impression? I wouldn't want to invest any time or money with him if I were a customer, regardless of how great he was at what he did!

"What would you think if someone handed you your business card"

Ask yourself whether the quality of your literature reflects the market position you want to occupy. If not, change it today! We will further examine the role that your literature plays in creating a positive image in a later chapter, but for now you need to be aware of how vital that first exposure to your brand.

Expensive Mistake

I know a small businessman who ordered 10,000 full-color direct mail pieces to send to prospective customers who lived within his target market. He had recently moved to the area and wanted to introduce his business to the community. He offered a free all-you-can-eat pizza feast, complete with breadsticks and soft drinks at his open house, along with many wonderful door prizes. He listed all his products and services and offered several specials for customers who signed up for his services at the open house. He had purchased an expensive list that gave him only the best-qualified leads for his business.

The folks on the list made at least X dollars and drove X cars and lived in X neighborhood- all the right stuff! He hired a local mail room company to address and stamp each piece, then prepared his staff for what was sure to be a gigantic influx of phone calls and walk-ins on the day the piece was to hit mailboxes.

The day finally came, and went, without so much as a single phone call. He waited and waited and waited. Four days went by before the first call came in, and the person said, *"Is this the business that's offering the free pizza party? I would like to take advantage of your specials! But I must tell you, it sure was difficult getting ahold of you...Your business name, address and phone number weren't listed in your mailing."*

Even though he had put in a lot of time and effort, not to mention money, he had forgotten to add him name, address and phone number- a very expensive mistake! Simple Rule #212- Always have several sets of eyeballs proofread any marketing materials a customer sees. This can prevent a lot of simple-to-correct mistakes.

2-Curb Appeal

For those of you who have a storefront, or run your business out of your home, the curb appeal is one of the categories of marketing. This was discussed in detail in the High Voltage Branding chapter.

3-Website

Today, nearly every business must be on the Internet in some form. Either a website, a blog, a YouTube channel, a social media platform, or similar. The term "curb appeal" can apply to this category as well. There are many companies that offer simply software programs that allow you to have a site up and running in a matter of minutes if needed. Or, if you are not tech-savvy, you can choose to hire a professional webmaster to build a beautiful site for you.

The cost of having a custom site has dropped like a lead balloon as the influx of talented web designers have entered the work force.

Long gone are the days where you needed to spend thousands of dollars to get a functional multi-page site online.

Aside from marketing, the Internet is a wonderful sales tool as well. In fact, there is a new breed of entrepreneurs who are making 100% of their revenues online without ever meeting a customer or handing out a price list. These folks put all their focus into their website, sales funnels, social media marketing, and e-mail databases in order to generate their sales dollars. It is a fast-growing industry, and many of these businesses do not have the foundational business acumen that most other businesses require in order to be successful.

I know two individuals who have a grand total of zero experience running a business and know nothing about sales, marketing, branding or any other business skills- yet are making huge amounts of money with their online business. Having been in business for over 30 years, my guess is that many of these online businesses will be short lived, and will be replaced with other short-lived online businesses, and they will be replaced with other short-lived online businesses…

It is still important that you have a certain level of business know-how in order to have staying power in business, not just a get-rich-quick scheme, whether you have a physical storefront or have a virtual storefront.

4-Advertising

Advertising is the most expensive type of marketing. This category includes direct mail, Facebook Ads, Google AdWords, newspapers, direct mail pieces, magazines, radio, TV, Little League banners, mall display space. It's the type of outreach that you must pay someone to conduct on your behalf. Advertising is considered passive marketing, because it doesn't require you to become personally involved in the success or failure of the program.

You can easily get sucked into advertising in every form, but without careful monitoring, you'll eat money faster than you can eat a pig at a pig roast. A word of caution- regardless of the type of advertising you engage in, you must make sure it fits into your overall goals and objectives for your business. Many businesses have disappeared due to overzealous advertising campaigns, so make sure you have your ducks in a row before jumping into expensive advertising.

5-Pricing

Once a potential customer believes something, it's tough to change their minds. The prices that you choose are also a form of marketing. If you are cheap, you are marketing. If you are the most expensive, you are also marketing. More on this topic in the Pricing chapter.

6-Press Releases

If you can inspire people to talk about you, there is little need to pay people to talk about you. All you need to do is tell the media something about you that might happen, has happened, or will happen. Let the local media know that you hired on a new office manager, won a prestigious award, expanded your business, added new products or services, or are hosting some sort of event.

"Editors are constantly looking for any newsworthy item for the business section"

You can let them know if you were invited to speak at a convention, association meeting, published a new book, or have even donated to a local non-profit charity. These are all legitimate reasons to write a press release. If you think that certain businesses are constantly being mentioned in the local newspaper and in the Chamber newsletter, you are probably right!

If you want to be considered an expert, you must look and sound like one. If nobody has appointed you the expert, appoint yourself! Blow your own horn! Your goal is to create awareness for your business, which in turn will lead to an increased value for your products and services. If you can generate more interest, why not try it?

7-Time

We are all on equal footing when it comes to time. We each have the same 24-hours in our day, no matter who we are. The topic of time is investigated in-depth in the Time Management chapter. Is one of your hooks that you are open for business at night? How about available on weekends when most people are off? The way you use your time can be an effective marketing tool, if done correctly.

8-Referral Networks

The referral network is your biggest ally. It's your most powerful marketing resource, and it can take your business to levels never dreamed of. After all, referred customers spend more money, are generally happier, stay with you longer, and come to you already sold. Let's talk about the types of referral networks that you can build.

Other Professionals

This first network is made up of other professionals that are in the same industry, or a complementary industry, as yours. This could be a supply house, another business professional that belongs to your local networking group like a Chamber of Commerce, or a personal acquaintance that knows the quality service you provide. Not only can they be an excellent source of referrals, you can also partner with them in cross-promotions.

You may have already partnered with a strong group like this, or maybe you haven't invested much time or effort into developing this circle of peers. In either case, I challenge you to sit down with a pen and paper and brainstorm until you come up with a list of other businesses you would like to develop a more substantial relationship with.

Once you've created your list, there are some simple things you can do to get the ball rolling. You can mail an invitation to a special Open House at your place of business to discuss the mutually beneficial aspects of partnering together. During this event, you can exchange information to become better educated about each other. You can also pick up the phone and give them a call or go visit them at their place of business. I guarantee they are just as interested in cracking the marketing code as you are! This kind of networking doesn't cost you anything but some time but can bring huge results.

Past & Present Customers

The second type of referral network, and by far the most neglected, is comprised of our past and present customers. You probably have hundreds if not thousands of past customers in your database who know and trust you, have already purchased from you, and are probably willing to do business with you again if given a compelling reason. And what are you doing with these happy customers? Their positive testimonies are largely untapped, and their ability to refer other new customers still on virgin soil.

If you aren't already taking advantage of your customers' testimonials to earn new referrals, you can begin today! Create a short questionnaire to give or mail to your customers. Offer them some sort of a bonus if they are willing to refer their family and friends to you. Be sure that the questionnaire asks them to rate your total experience so you have an idea on areas where you can stand some improvement.

Stay away from questionnaires that allow people to simply give a number or check a box. You want them to have to write an answer. You want to obtain as much information as possible from them, so ask them to write out their answers in descriptive terms. At the bottom of the form, ask for names, addresses and phone numbers of friends or family who might be interested in doing business with you. Then send them an offer they can't refuse via e-mail, mail, in person, or via your current customers.

"Whatever you do, strike while the iron is hot! If you wait too long, the afterglow will diminish"

The entire sales and marketing games are built on creating positive emotions, and you will lose momentum if you wait too long. The best marketers understand this dynamic and develop the emotional trappings to guarantee a fantastic experience. If a customer says to you, *"Man, we love what you do and are happy to be doing business with you"*, ask them to put that in writing! Testimonials are KING and make getting them a top priority.

On this note, keep in mind that there are only two kinds of service: great and bad. Mediocrity makes little or no impression on most people. Make it your goal to go above and beyond the call of duty when it comes to providing gold-medal, top-notch, number-one-rated customer service. This is the best way to create customer for life and to keep the referral highway filled with traffic.

There is no better form of marketing than the existence of a happy customer list, along with a referral network of other professionals. If you get this right, you will never have to spend money on expensive advertising ever again.

9-E-mail Database/Direct Mail Marketing

While the short-term goal of a marketing campaign is to get customers to come to you for the first time, the overall goal is to keep them coming back time and time again over a long period of time. If you have done a good job of collecting data from your customers, this database is priceless! Keep in touch with them on a regular basis so that you have "top of mind awareness" with your past customers. Sending a consistent e-mail newsletter or mailing them a special offer or Gift Card will keep limit the amount of dollars you spend outside of this circle.

10-Phone Calls/Website Visitors

The goals of any effective campaign are to get the phone to ring or to drive a prospect to your website, right? If this doesn't happen, all the marketing in the world is useless. But do you understand how much it costs to make your phone ring, or to get a visitor to your website?

Understanding the Costs

If you already track each call that comes in, this exercise will be easy for you. If you don't you will need to track every call that comes in for a period, let's say one week for starters. Calls from your family or the pizza shop don't count! Create a log sheet with columns for each of the different sources of leads that you get. We covered this potential list earlier. W

When you have tallied your incoming calls, divide your total marketing expense by the number of calls your received. You might be surprised by the amount. I've heard numbers as low as $1.25 per customer and as much as $3600 per customer. This is not an exact approach, but it will give you an idea on where your best results are coming from, and what money is not bringing you the return.

Do the same with your Internet advertising. Divide the number of online orders by the amount of advertising dollars spent over a period. Many of you already know this number down to the exact penny, many of you do not.

Your Voice Mail

When your customers reach your voice mail, what do they hear? I want you to listen to your message right now. I've surveyed hundreds of businesses around the world to determine what their recordings sounded like, and here is the winner-

"Hello, thank you for calling XYZ. If you've reached this recording during our normal business hours, we are busy with another customer or on the other line. Please leave us your name, number and reason for your call, and we will give you a call back at our earliest convenience. Thank you for calling and have a nice day!"

Does your message sound like this? Don't worry, you are not alone! Do you think that our customers get sick and tired of hearing the same words regardless of who they are calling? So, why not add a little character and pizazz to the mix? Have some enthusiasm, exhibit some sincerity, and have some excitement in your voice!

There are several things that you should pay attention to when listening to your message. Does it sound tinny and far away? Is there the proper amount of enthusiasm in the voice? Are the words spoken clearly and concisely, or does it sound rushed and uncaring?

There is nothing worse than calling another business only to encounter a voice message in which the speaker sound bored, irritated, and disgusted. It makes me not want to do business with them! Make sure that your own message is friendly, spirited, and welcoming. This is something you can do right now if you choose. Grab a piece of paper, write out a new script, and record your new voicemail!

Answering the Phone

The same rules apply when you answer the phone in person. You want to sound approachable, trustworthy, professional and upbeat. A simple *"Good morning. This is Bob, how can I help you today?"* is a good start. If you use your first name, the caller is much more likely to give you their first name as well without you having to ask for it. And once you have their first name, use it!

People feel important and special when they hear their name, and it makes a conversation more personable. Ask the needed questions, then shut up! The best way to show a customer that you care and value them is to listen. Hear them out, we were given one mouth and two ears for a reason!

Treat each call that comes like gold. These calls pay the bills, pays your employees, and pays you! If you have a staff person who handles most of the incoming calls, make sure they fully understand that it's your image on the line every time they pick up the receiver and say hello. The phone is your opportunity to make a positive impression on potential customers, and there is not a second chance to make a first impression.

A Few Ways to Promote Your Business

Price Lists	**Websites**	**Pens**
Brochures	**Internet ads**	**Bumper stickers**
Flyers	**Magazine Ads**	**Calendars**
Business Cards	**Search Engines**	**Newspaper Ads**
Direct Mail	**Signage**	**Gift Certificates**
Merchant Co-Op	**Billboards**	**Welcome Wagons**
Slide Shows	**Gift Cards**	**Videos**
Auto Wraps	**Mall Displays**	**Charity Events**
Table Tents	**Business Displays**	**Church Directories**
Bookmarks	**Promo Raffles**	**Business Fairs**
Newsletters	**County Fairs**	**Referral Programs**
Affiliate Programs	**Telemarketing**	**Yellow Pages**
Google AdWords	**Facebook Ads**	**Vendor Programs**
Networking	**Key Chains**	**Coffee Mugs**
Radio Ads	**Note Pads**	**Window Displays**
TV Commercials	**Magnets**	**Hot Air Balloons**
Pencils	**T-Shirts**	**Banners**

BUT REMEMBER- The #1 way to get business is to take care of your current customers and ask them for referrals!

Final Thoughts

We have so many choices when it comes to making a purchase. There are three grades of gasoline, ten types of milk, ten types of batteries, three sizes of fries, and twenty kinds of toothpaste! Some people only the buy the most expensive, and some people only buy the cheapest. Regardless of what you are selling, someone else is selling it cheaper, better, and faster. Why would they pay you more for your products and services? Because of your perceived value. They need to think they will get more from you than the other guy, and if you don't already believe in yourself, who would anyone else?

Ultimately, the key to great marketing is you must be heard. If you have something great but don't have the means to let people know about it, you will fail. You want people to talk about you and be able to easily find you.

And keep in mind that this is not optional- you cannot not market, just like you cannot not answer the phone. like you cannot not answer the phone. If someone calls and you answer, you are marketing. If you don't answer, you are still marketing.

Chapter 5

Sales Magic

Marketing and branding are big challenges for sure, but they are only the first steps in building a successful business. Once you have gotten prospective customers interested in your blue widget you need to translate that interest into purchases. That's where the selling comes in.

With solid sales skills, you'll be able to convert more phone calls and website inquiries into paying customers and take your sales averages to places never dreamed of (And most importantly, you'll be that much closer to creating the lifestyle of your dreams). Without good sales skills, the marketing in the world will be a total and complete waste! You need to either learn how to be a top-notch salesperson (there are TONS of resources to teach you how) or hire someone else to do it for you. It's that simple.

Marketing? Selling? What's the Difference?

This is an important foundational understanding for your business- and I want to make sure we have our foundation poured before we build our house. In my view, marketing is everything you do up until the phone rings or a visitor checks out your website. Sales is everything that happens after that.

Sales Makes the World Go Around

The whole world's economy revolves around the buying and selling of products and services. From Wall Street to Main Street, our lives are built on the buying and selling principle.

The Life of a Dozen Eggs

Think about it. You meander into the grocery store on a Sunday afternoon to do your weekly shopping and you buy lots of stuff. Let's say one of those items is a carton of a dozen eggs. When you purchase your carton, that effectively ends the sales process for that particular dozen eggs, but let's work backwards and see what the process entailed.

To begin with, some broker had to sell the store those eggs, Then, there was a farm out there that sold the eggs to the broker's company. For the farmer to be able to collect those eggs, he had to have all the right equipment to handle the eggs with care and to guarantee the health of those eggs. Each of those pieces of equipment was bought and sold by someone- as were all the parts and materials required to build the equipment and so on, and so on.

Those eggs came from chickens. For the chickens to lay eggs, the farmer had to have a rooster, who needs to eat something (as do the chickens!). So, the farmer had to buy grain and pellets and sterilized water, which means somebody had to sell those products to him. And then there is the actual carton that the eggs go into. All the raw materials that go into making that carton must come from somewhere, which means somebody and buy and sell each of them.

If we were talking about cardboard, each of the ingredients was probably bought and sold five or six times going back to when a single tree was standing tall amongst its brothers and sisters in an ancient forest.

All of this buying and selling takes place just so you can go to the store, spend $1.50, and buy a dozen eggs to make egg salad sandwiches, or a cake, or breakfast, or a souffle…and then you'll also need to buy flour, and sugar, and-

Phew……I need to sit down and rest!

If something as simple as a dozen eggs requires that much buying and selling, just think about things such as a jumbo jet, or x-ray machines, or computers. Whether you like it or not, you are in the business of selling, plain and simple.

Buying Is Based on Benefits

People are going to buy things…but they also have a lot of choices. So why do people buy the things they do? As we discussed in the High Voltage Branding chapter it's partly because of the image that we create around our business. They also do it because of the benefits they will receive in some way- it may feed their family, make them feel better about themselves, improve their perceived social standing, etc...

The greater the benefits, the more they are motivated to buy, and the more they will buy. If you can increase your customers' perception of the benefits of buying from you, it will equate to dollars in your bank account.

An Emotional Response

Sales are typically emotionally driven, then justified logically. Believe it or not, the emotional benefits are what motivates most purchases (outside necessities like food).

Think back to the most recent big-ticket item you purchased for your family- whether it was a car, a new big TV, a boat, or something else that required some serious thought before deciding.

- Why did you make the purchase?
- What were you thinking before you made the purchase?
- What were you thinking during the purchase?
- What was the deciding factor?
- How did it differ from your original concept?
- How did you feel after the purchase?
- What type of follow-up did you receive?
- What was your budget for this purchase beforehand?
- How much did you actually spend?
- Did you end up buying additional features that you didn't figure on before making the initial decision?
- How did you feel once it was completed? Did you have feelings of guilt, or did you justify in your head all the reasons why it was okay to spend what you did?

If you are like most people, quality and price won't be listed among your top motivators. People don't buy for quality and price; they buy for the benefits. They may make a purchase to gain the benefits of high quality (a luxury car may be more reliable and impress your friends), but once there are enough benefits established, price becomes secondary.

People who are motivated enough will buy just about anything in this world. If you can keep that in the front of your mind as you spend some time immersed in the sales thought process, you will be miles ahead of the game!

Here's the trick…benefits are extremely personal and vary from customer to customer. That's where the job of a salesperson comes into play.

Start with The Right Atmosphere

There is a subtle difference between successful and unsuccessful salespeople. The unsuccessful salesperson attempts to sell whatever it is they have. The successful salesperson creates an atmosphere that makes the customer want to buy whatever you are selling.

Have you ever gone to a restaurant with high expectations, only to have them crushed as soon as you walked in the door? If so, you probably didn't spend as much as you might have- you skipped dessert or didn't order a second glass of wine.

Conversely, have you wandered into a restaurant without any expectations and walked away with a tremendous experience? Some of my most expensive dinners have been at places where I was pleasantly surprised by the tantalizing appetizers, delicious meals and desserts, extensive wine list, relaxing ambience, and service that was second to none.

At that point, it didn't really matter what the price was, did it? The experience and the emotion became much more powerful than the price of a bottle of wine.

Remember this: People don't like to be sold, but they love to buy! I don't know about you, but when I get in the car and head down to the local store to make some sort of purchase, I have an exciting feeling of exuberance and anticipation. Whether it's a new car, a pair of Levi's, or just the makings for one of my BBQ feasts, I have a great time and have an emotional reaction. Often, I will spend more than I had anticipated before I left home, and my guess is that you have had similar experiences.

Why? Because something in the way the products are packaged, or displayed, or designed made us want to buy them- made us feel the benefits of owning them. The next time you go out shopping, try to think of the reasons why you purchase the things you do. It's a fun exercise!

Why Should Customers Choose You?

Before we go any further, let's take an inventory of your sales tools and see where you currently are with your understanding of the sales process. To start, I want to ask you a very important question- and it's probably the most important question you can ever ask yourself about your business:

Why you?

I want you to think of specific reasons why a prospective customer would choose you instead of anybody else. Why do customers buy from you? Why are you better than your competitors? Keep in mind that it's not enough to list why you are *as good* as your competitors, you must know why you are better. If you must stumble around to come up with that answer, your customers and prospects will interpret that as insecurity and doubt. In today's fiercely competitive marketplace, there must be something besides the quality of what you do that give people a compelling reason to spend their dough with you.

I want you to be specific with this next exercise. Take just a few minutes right now and scratch out some thoughts on paper. Dig deep and come up with three reasons why people should spend a portion of their expendable income with you.

Here are the beginnings of a few sentences that may give you some direction:

I am the only one who….

I am unique because….

Our prices are higher because….

My customers come to me because….

My prices are better than our competitors because….

Okay kids, how did we do? You may have been able to write down ten reason, which is fantastic! Or you may have sat there for most of the time thinking intently and coming up with next to nothing. Either way, it completely okay. We will get you there, eventually!

This question- why you? - must be answered before you will be ready to become a powerhouse sales dynamo for your business. Over the next couple of days, give it some more of your bandwidth.

The Power Selling Self-Test

While you are sitting there with pen in hand, this would be a great time to dive into our next exercise. I want you to grade yourself on a scale of 1 to 10, with 10 being the highest. There are no pass or fail scores, and you will not be graded. It is simply information, and the more useful information you can have about yourself, the more prepared you will be to tackle the challenges and obstacles that appear along the road to success. Here we go!

1- Do you have a comprehensive sales strategy- beginning with the first phone call/website visit and ending when the lifetime value of that customer ends? If so, what is it?

2- Do you feel you are maximizing each order that you write as far as dollar amount?

3- What are your sales averages for each of your products and services?

4- How do you feel about your sales skills on the phone? Can you/your staff answer questions effectively, build a bond, then get them to commit?

5- Do you have incentives built into your price list that encourage customers to spend more?

6- Do you have confidence that your price list is your #1 salesperson?

7- Are you able to overcome objections easily and effectively?

8- Do you have a system for follow-up after purchase? What is it?

9- Do you have a referral program in place that motivates customers to send you new business? What is it?

10- Do you offer incentive-driven packages in your price list that act as a silent salesperson? What are the incentives?

Let's switch gears just a little bit and think about the following statements. These can be answered with a simple yes or no.

- I feel good about myself and feel confident in my sales skill sets.
- I usually say the right thing at the right time.
- People seek out my company.
- I don't seem to get too discouraged, even if I fail repeatedly.
- I am an excellent listener.
- I can read people's body language with ease.
- I can see many ways to define a problem and understand the causes.
- I am skilled at drawing out other people's concerns and problems.
- I manage my time so well that I can accomplish everything that is important in a typical workday.
- I focus on the big picture goals for my business rather than always reacting to whatever the "crisis of the day" is.
- I keep looking for ways to be more effective and productive.
- I don't care how long it takes to succeed at a task, because I know I'll succeed in the end.

And we are done! How did it go? This was only an exercise, but I encourage you to take some time and expand on the answers that you came up with…especially if you noted areas where you can make improvements. Even if you aren't a born salesperson, you can learn the basic principles of powerful sales techniques and become a sales superstar!

The Secret Is You

There's no quick fix or magic wand I can wave, no potion I can give you to create the level of success you are dreaming of in your life and your business. There is, however, a secret formula that I'm about to give you. I've spent most of my life searching for this mystical mathematical formula that I'm going to share with you now. Grab a pen and get ready for me to rock your world. Are you ready? Come a little closer…. closer. Okay, here it is…

There isn't any secret formula. There's just you, and the power of your thoughts. Here is what the best salespeople sell- in order of importance:

1- Themselves

2- Their company

3- Their products and services

4- Their price

Average or below average salespeople do things the opposite way:

1- Their price

2- Their products and services

3- Their company

4- Themselves

When it comes down to it, customers buy you first, way before they can buy your company or your products. If they like brand "you", then they will be more likely to buy anything you have to sell.

Shared Traits

All successful salespeople have several traits in common. If these descriptions sound like you, great. If not, there may be areas where you can focus on strengthening your skills and boosting your confidence.

The best salespeople:

1- Associate with other positive, encouraging, and successful people. They stay away from those who bring them down or constantly complain- people who never seem to get anywhere. Invest your time building relationships with other successful people- people who have the same aspirations as you do and want to make a difference in the world.

2- Keep abreast of the newest and hottest ideas. How much time do you spend each day reading a new book, trying new ideas out, or even just watching a new show on TV? New information is the lifeblood for you to grow and become a better version of who you are today. You can bet that your competition is keeping their eyes open, and so are your customers. Open your mind and look around you. See what other people are doing. You must have a steady diet of change and innovation in order to keep the edge of your sword sharp.

3- Set and work towards goals. Decide what you want, then get started attaining those goals. Don't just talk about it, do it! Along with education, setting goals is the surest method I know to set yourself on a course of happiness. If you don't develop the hunger and courage to pursue your goals, you will lose your nerve and give up. Do you spend quality time each day setting and reviewing your goals? In the evening, my mind is mush, so I make a point of waking up early every day which is when I get my best work done. There are no phone calls, no kids to take care of, no people…just me and my brain (and a good cup of coffee, of course!)

4- Make the most of every opportunity. They take advantage of opportunities that come their way. We've all heard people say, *"Boy, she sure is lucky!"* or *"He seems to get all the lucky breaks!"* But luck isn't random, it's the result of hard work, perseverance and dedication. When an opportunity arises, you must also be able to recognize it (often it shows up in the form of adversity) then act on it. It often seems to be very elusive but exists all over. Very few can see it because it usually requires change, which is a very scary thought.

5- Take risks and make mistakes. Taking chances is a very common thread among the ultra-successful business minds in the world. I'm not talking about crazy risks that jeopardized their entire empire, but rather measured risks that they can live with. It may hurt, but the benefits far outweigh any potential negative impact. Thomas Edison failed over 6,000 times before he finally invented the light bulb, and Barry Bonds struck out more times than anyone else in history (he also has hit more home runs than anyone ever!) I don't think for one minute that we would call these people failures, would we? The best teacher I ever had was failure- and believe me, I've had my fair share of that. If you learn to look at mistakes that you make and failures you have had as learning experiences, it puts a whole new perspective on things.

Free-Association Exercises

Before we move on to defining each step of the selling process, we are going to do some free-association exercises. I want you to use your spoken voice for this- speak the words out loud! Don't worry about making mistakes, I simply want you to do the best that you can.

1- Describe your favorite movie…

2- Describe the moon….

3- Describe a set of keys….

4- Describe love….

5- Describe anger….

6- Describe one of your products or services….

7- Describe the experience a customer will have with you….

We communicate facts, feelings, conviction, and emotion to our customers through the words we use. Being good at painting irresistible mental pictures, is one of the best skills you can have. Doing this means adding vivid details into your sales presentation. Choosing the right words helps to convey your passion, your enthusiasm, and the zest and zeal you have for your craft.

I recommend writing out a list of all products and services you offer. Then, come up with a paragraph or two that describes each one in vivid and colorful detail, colorful. In fact, why don't you do that before you begin the next chapter!

Let's establish a make-believe business that we can use for example purposes throughout this chapter. We will call it John Doe's Studios. We can start by describing a wedding album that he sells in his business.

Not so good example…

At John Doe Studios, your wedding album will include about 50 images, some in color, some in black and white. These will be selected from throughout your wedding day. You can pick the color of the album cover and add whatever text you want.

Much better example….

Each John Doe studios wedding album is elegantly designed to tell the story of your special day with all its beauty and romance. We will combine breathtaking color and black-and-white images with meaningful words to produce an album that will make you laugh and bring tears to your eyes- an album that is as unique as you are.

Another Big Secret Revealed

I have been to countless seminars and workshops, read hundreds of books, listen to umpteen podcasts, watched numerous DVD's, and spent time with some of the best and richest salespeople in the entire world. After exposing myself to all that education, here's what I can tell you. There are thousands of ways to do just about everything, thousands of different closing techniques, conversational ice breakers, different ways to overcome objections, to say hello on the phone, etc. It's very easy to become intimidated and overwhelmed with the overload of information. As a result, most people simply do nothing.

With that in mind, I have boiled every speck of knowledge that I have ever learned about successful selling into one little Golden and I am about to give you that secret so you can have unsurpassed sales success and wealth beyond your imagination. Here it is ... Be nice! That's it. People buy from people they like all the fancy techniques in the world won't amount to a hill of beans if your clients don't like you, so be nice!

THE SALES PROCESS

Mmmmm…. Cheese!

If you like cheese as much as I do, then you probably have had the opportunity at some point to visit a factory where they make cheese. One of my favorite places is the Tillamook cheese factory in Tillamook, Oregon. You walk in and are immediately overcome by the immensity and grandness of the building. If you want, you can take a guided tour behind the scenes and hear about the entire process from beginning to end.

If you know anything about making cheese, you know it all starts with milk from a cow, and if you have ever been to Tillamook, there are cows everywhere! From there, exact ingredients, temperatures and aging are combined to give each type of cheese its distinctive flavor and texture. There are conveyor belts, and cheese cutters, wrappers, boxers, stackers and loaders, and quality control personnel making sure that every single block of cheese meets rigorous standards.

At the end, big boxes are loaded onto a big truck and then carried away to the retail stores where you and I can go in, by the block of cheese and take it home to enjoy! They definitely have their systems down; every step along the way is controlled by a process- and at the end of that process, a marvelous block of cheese is produced that taste exactly like the block of cheese you bought last week at the store. However, if any part of the system fails, the cheese doesn't make it to our bellies.

Just like making a good block of cheese requires a specific process, you should have a well-planned system in place for selling your products and services.

The Pre-Sell

The pre-sell is everything that you do before a perspective customer contacts you. Your marketing, networking, the professionalism of your marketing Arsenal, your advertising, word of mouth, the irresistibility of your offers, your relationships with people throughout your community- all these things go into creating value for what you do. Together, they comprise the first step in creating an effective sales atmosphere.

Earlier, I mentioned that people make judgments about you within the first 5 seconds after they are exposed to your voice, your signage, your business card, your physical appearance, your answering machine, etc. That 5 seconds will either help you build value, or it will take it away.

Perception is reality; we all make decisions in our subconscious minds about what kind of value something has for our life and how much we are willing to spend for that value. If you want to be viewed as someone worth spending a lot of money on, every aspect of your brand must be top notch.

The Initial Contact
On the Phone:

Our initial contact with a perspective customer usually occurs on the phone, and I would venture to say that, for most of you, taking phone calls is not your favorite thing to do. You didn't get into the business of being an entrepreneur because you liked talking on the phone, did you? However, this is the first real opportunity for you to sell yourself, educate the prospect about what they can expect from you, and begin to build a long-term relationship with him. Understanding that the telephone is one of the most important, if not the most important, selling tool that you have will help you begin to look at it a little differently. After all, when a call comes into your business, it means your marketing has done its job and now it's time to begin the sales process.

The first rule to follow is that you always want to be smiling and happy when you answer the phone, even if you are having a bad day. People can sense positive energy and negative vibes through the telephone, so take a deep breath before answering the phone and show your best side. We all have bad days now and then, but you should never let that come across on the phone. As soon as the phone is answered it's game time! The goal is to get them excited about you and the experience they are going to have.

Questions About Pricing:

It doesn't matter what country you live in, whether you are in the far reaches of the earth or are in downtown Metropolisville, we all get the same questions during our first phone call. How much? Since you know that 99% of all prospects are going to ask that question, wouldn't it make sense to have some sort of script figured out ahead of time instead of trying to spontaneously come up with an answer?

In many cases, your answers may be questions- questions that help you better understand the prospects needs. After all, people ask about price because they don't know what else to ask. What they really want to know, though, is whether you are the right business for them. Are you going to be able to meet their needs? That's what they really want to know ... But the only question they can think of is "how much?"

Imagine if you walked into a friend's jewelry store and they said, "Hey, would you do me a favor and watch the store for a few minutes while I go to the bank and make a deposit?"

The phone hasn't rung all day, but if it does go ahead and answer it and do the best that you can. You agree, and he leaves you all alone with $1,000,000 worth of jewelry comma and the phone.

Suddenly, the phone rings, so you answer it and a nice young man on the other end of the phone asks, how much are your diamond rings? What do you say? At this point you have no useful information for him because you know nothing about diamonds- but can you think of some questions to ask him? How about:

#1- What size diamond are you looking for?

#2- Is it for a woman or a man?

#3- What type of cut do you want?

#4- What type of setting do you want? Gold? Platinum?

#5- Do you need the ring by certain date?

#6- Would you like the ring delivered or would you prefer to pick it up?

#7- Do you have a budget in mind for the ring?

That wasn't so hard, was it? In fact, there are probably many more questions you can think of off the top of your head. So why is it when somebody asks how much we charge for one of our products and services, we break into a cold sweat and our stomach starts to churn? Why do we feel that we need to give them some sort of solid answer before we have any additional information? The biggest mistake that most businesspeople make is they try to sell every single product they have when on the phone, and as a result they never really find out what the customer wants.

Price is usually part of the conversation, but rarely is it the deciding factor as to whether the prospect will come to you and do business. So, if price isn't going to be part of the deciding factor for them, then don't you make it the stumbling block! Your ability to discuss pricing confidently is directly related to your strength and belief in yourself and your products. If you don't have faith that your product is worth every penny, you won't be able to sell it. A little later, we will dive into some meat and potatoes techniques for handling objections over the phone.

Additional Tips

Here are some quick-hitting concepts that you should remember about the initial contact, whether it be in person or on the phone.

#1- Always speak with a clear and professional voice, show confidence in yourself, your prices and your system. If you sound and act confident, that will rub off on your prospect and they will turn into a customer very quickly.

#2- When asked about your prices, do not give specifics, give ranges. Once you have qualified your prospect and know what it is that they are looking for, it will become easier to give them specific prices, but to begin with only give out ranges. It doesn't matter what industry you are in, this technique works for them all.

#3- Planting the seeds of money with everything you say is also a big part of the emotionally-driven sales process.

#4- Use qualifying questions to establish the needs, budget, and desires of your customer.

#5- Accept the fact that not everybody is meant to be your customer. Once you have a solid idea about what a prospect is looking for, if you don't feel they fit into your game plan, it's OK to send them down the road. Not everyone is meant to be your customer, it's OK to just say no.

The Ping-Pong Exercise

Let's take some time right now to do what I call the ping-pong exercise, which will give you a firm grasp on how to handle initial contacts on the phone or in person. The initial conversation is usually just like a tennis match or a ping-pong game, with several volleys back and forth. This exercise is intended to begin for you the process of creating powerful scripts that can be used anytime, anywhere.

I'm going to give you some examples of statements that prospects all over the world seemed to ask over the phone, And I want you to write down how you would respond to each one period this will be the beginning of your phone script. I highly recommend you come back to this exercise later today and give it some more thought- but for right now, go ahead and jot down some short answers. Ready?

#1- How much are your blue widgets?

#2- Can you mail me some information?

#3- I will think about it and call you back.

#4- The guy down the street is a lot less than you are!

#5- Wow! Your prices are the most expensive I have ever heard of!

You may have encountered some questions, or stalls, other than the ones I have mentioned here, so take a minute right now to write those down, then note how you will respond.

Now we're going to switch gears. I want you to make a list of questions that you will ask. Here are some ideas to get you started

#1- How did you happen to hear about us?

#2- Do you have a budget for your blue widget?

#3- Would you consider getting a package of blue widgets if the price was right?

#4- When are you looking to make your final decision?

#5- What will you be using your blue widget for?

I hope this exercise got your creative mojo working and started you thinking about how you deal with prospects on the phone, or in person. Thinking along these lines will help you access information about what the customer is looking for and will get them talking about themselves- which keeps things on an emotional level. The more you can get them to talk, the more emotionally attracted they will become to you. Again, we are in the business of selling emotion. If you can do that, the sales will follow.

Once the sale is made, there are a couple of other things you can do to continue to build your relationship.

Write a thank you note within 24 hours after the customer makes their purchase. Or, a quick phone call 24 hours after. Are your competitors doing this? Do you want to swim in a red ocean with everyone else, all fighting over the same customers with the same products and services? Or do you want to create a blue ocean where you are the only swimmer in the sea?

In the end, people won't remember what you did or what you said, they will remember how you made them feel. Passion is the fulcrum point of all sales. If you show passion during your relationship with your customers, that emotion will transfer to them, and will create a desire in their hearts to buy. Passion is an emotional feeling that is like the mumps- it's very contagious!

Features & Benefits

Remember back when you were a kid riding around all summer on your bike without a care in the world? Nothing bothered you and life was good. You probably even had a family-run pizza joint down at the corner like I did. I can remember on Friday nights how my entire family would all meet down there at dinner time to enjoy a big slab of pizza and some sodas.

My favorite part was when my mom gave me quarters so I could play the pinball machines in between slices. If I ran out, she always seemed to have more. Moms are always good for change, you know. There was an endless supply of quarters coming from the bottom of my mom's purse, at least it seemed that way.

Looking back, I can see that it wasn't necessarily the pizza that got my attention- it was the pinball. That was something that benefited me directly, and I was thoroughly enjoying my time on the flippers. The feature, so to speak, was the pizza. The benefit was the pinball.

Now that I'm a big kid, I don't get to ride around on my bike all summer and I sure don't get to play pinball very often. But I do understand the value of features and benefits and how they play an integral role in the sales process. All products and services have features and benefits, but it's the benefits that motivate people to act, and to buy.

Think about it. Why did you purchase your last car? It probably had all sorts of cool features and modern amenities, but when it came down to it, the benefits of those features are what got you nailed down. It had antilock brakes, which would keep you and the kids safe on those rainy nights. It had a DVD player in the back, which made it convenient to travel with young children on long trips. It had an extra-large cargo space, which meant that everybody in the family could put their suitcase in.

It had a surround sound speaker system, which meant everyone could enjoy the music. It had a moon roof, so you could stare into the Sky on those warm summer nights. It had a 6-cylinder engine, which was strong enough to tow a boat but small enough to give you respectable gas mileage. You didn't buy the DVD player, or the moonroof, or the six-cylinder engine or the speaker system. You bought the benefits and the value that those things brought to your life.

Let's take this a bit further. What about the features and benefits of a ballpoint pen?

Feature: It has a clicker on the end that retracts the tip.

Benefit: You won't accidentally get ink all over your shirt

Feature: It has black ink

Benefit: You can sign all your legal documents with it

Feature: It has a metal clip on the side so you can put it in your shirt

Benefit: It won't fall out when you bend over

How about a cup of coffee?

Feature: It has a handle on the side

Benefit: If you are drinking something hot, you won't burn your hands

Feature: It holds 8 ounces of fluid

Benefit: The contents won't get cold before you drink it all

Feature: It's white

Benefit: It will go with just about any color you may have on your table.

Now, take your products and services and develop a list of features and benefits. This alone will make you a powerhouse to be reckoned with!

Eliminating Risk

Eliminating risk is another important factor in determining your customers desire to purchase. If you can eliminate the risk in their eyes, they are much more likely to buy big. How much simpler can selling get, you ask? In order to harness the power of this strategy, ask yourself these questions:

1- In the eyes of my customers, what risks are they taking when they make a purchasing decision?

2- How can I remove that risk during the sales process?

A risk is usually just a mental barrier that causes people to hesitate. As a professional salesperson, your number one job is to identify the risks, then eliminate them as you go along, so you need to be an expert at risk removal. Nobody likes taking risks, but everybody wants the reward that risks bring with it.

If the risk is the price, then the reward is the value. One at a time, brick by brick, remove the risks that the buyer perceives as stopping them from doing business with you. Then drive home the rewards, both logically and emotionally.

Overcoming Objections and Closing

If you hear things like , let me think about it and I'll get back to you later, let me talk it over with my spouse and I'll call you tomorrow, or I can get the same thing cheaper down the street, you are losing many potential customers each month , and needlessly so.

In fact, a good salesperson becomes welcomes those types of objections because they see them as opportunities to build value in their product. And, as luck would have it, there are time-tested responses that can easily turn objections into more customers and bigger orders.

An Ounce of Prevention

When dealing with objections, prevention is always the best

medicine. Most objections can be overcome simply by addressing them as you go instead of waiting until the prospect brings it up. To do that, you must get real about your place in the market, as well as your perceived weaknesses and strengths. Either you are too big, too small, too new, too old, too far away, too expensive, etc. There will always be a reason why a prospect WON'T do business with you.

The tendency for us is to hide our weaknesses so that nobody can see them, but a better strategy is to minimize any weakness by turning it into a benefit- to turn your perceived weaknesses into the exact reason why they should do business with you.

For example, if your business is on the other end of town from the prospect, people might perceive this as a disadvantage, unless you directly address and eliminate this potential concern in your presentation hyphen

Mrs. Jones, although we may be further away than other businesses you may be considering, you will find our services very attentive, just like we were right next door!

Or, if your prospects are always saying they can get their blue widget for less money somewhere else, don't wait to hear it from them, beat them to the punch by justifying your higher prices during your presentation. Tell them why you are more expensive early on, which will eliminate that objection from the picture.

"Mrs. Jones, if you shop around long enough, you can always find someone who can meet your needs for a few dollars less. We don't claim to be the least expensive or the most expensive. But our customers have found that when choosing us, they get a greater value for their investment period they're getting a team of industry professionals and that saves money in the long run. Isn't that what you are really looking for?"

Track Objections and Planned Responses

Every day we hear the same objections repeatedly, yet we still show up to work each day with the same old stale techniques, just hoping and praying that today will be different. But it doesn't change. This will absolutely wear you down overtime!

Nobody likes to hear objections, because they make us feel like we aren't doing a good job. But when you have no objections, you have no sale because the customer isn't engaged. And when you have too many objections you also have no sales because the customer isn't convinced. Objections are, by their very nature, a mixed bag.

Here's a great exercise. Start writing down all the objections that you get on a regular basis for the next couple of weeks and listen to your prospects very carefully. Every time you hear an objection and don't get a sale, write it down. By the end of the two weeks you will be able to see a clear pattern emerge. It will tell you what part of your presentation is weak.

Based on this information you can pre-plan your responses. This will make your whole life a lot easier. In fact, studies show that salespeople who usually carefully plan out their responses make an average of four times more income than those who just make up their responses on the fly. That's an amazing amount! Realizing that your income and your lifestyle are directly related to your ability to overcome objections should be a good enough reason to overcome any discomfort you have with handling objections.

Best of all, very powerful and motivating responses to all

objections are already available to you. You don't have to reinvent the wheel to tackle this problem, you can just profit from other people's experiences.

Have faith, ye people! Objections are a sign of interest. They show that your prospect or customer is engaged in the sales process. Depending on what type of objection you get, each statement also helps you to understand exactly where you are in the sales process. Here are four steps to overcoming any objection.

#1- Neutralize or cushion the objection- What this basically means is that you agree with your customer. Use phrases like, *I understand how you feel, Mrs. Jones*, or *That makes perfect sense, or I totally agree with you*, or *I would feel the same way if I was in your shoes*. When a prospect or customer says something that could potentially be confrontational their defensive guard is always up, because they are expecting you to react in a negative way or not react at all.

#2- Repeat or restate the objection- For example if the objection is, I want to check around before I make a decision, you can say, *Mrs. Jones, I totally understand your need to make sure you are selecting the right business for your needs*. In that one sentence you have neutralized the objection by agreeing with them, then you have restated the objection back in a way that makes sense to them.

#3- Give them a reason to decide today- You could do this, in this scenario, by continuing with a statement like, *Mrs. Jones I totally understand your need to make sure you are selecting the right business for your needs, I heard that from many of our current customers before they selected us. But after checking around they found that we were best able to meet their individual needs and provide them with a wonderful experience.*

#4- Ask a closing question- Ask a question that gets them to agree with what you have said. For example, *Now isn't that what you are really looking for Mrs. Jones?*

Of course, you will need to add some of your own words, your own personal style, and practice the delivery so you are comfortable with the presentation, but by following these four simple steps, you would be able to book more business, generate more sales, and make your business more profitable.

More on Phone Skills

Earlier, I covered the main objections we hear on the phone, this happens on what seems like a daily basis. In fact, 8 out of 10 calls that come into your business with, "*Let me think about it or I'll get back to you*", you will never see again.

Experience shows that they will never call you back and you will never get a second chance to win their business. So, if you accept that excuse and let them go easily, you are losing 80% of your possible business! That means you need to do a better job of helping them overcome their indecision and get them excited about you and create a sense of urgency.

ADDITIONAL CLOSING TECHNIQUES

With literally thousands of closing techniques, it can be overwhelming if you try to eat the entire elephant all at one time. There are some basic strategies, however, that you can implement right away to put extra dollars in your bank account.

The Feel, Felt, Found Close- *This can be used for just about any objection you may hear. "Mrs. Jones, I understand how you* ***feel.*** *Many of our customers* ***felt*** *the same way before making the decision to come to us. But after they had a chance to experience our wonderful service and excellent products, they* ***found*** *us to offer the best value for their money. Isn't that what you're really looking for?*

The Boomerang Close- Turn an objection into an advantage. For an example, if the customer says that you are more expensive than everyone else, here's what you might say: *"Mrs. Jones that's the very reason why you should come to us. Although we may be a few dollars more, I am confident you will see why once you have a chance to experience our service, you all choose us. Any purchase you make comes with a 100% unconditional guarantee, so you never have to worry about that. So, we are less expensive in the long run than any of our competitors. I believe what you are really looking for is to get a great value for your investment, isn't that right? "*

The Minor Point/Alternative Close- This close, which offers only two options, is usually used when a customer is having a hard time deciding. It can get them off the fence and can add dollars to the order if done correctly basically whatever you want your customer to do should be the second of the two options. They will usually go with what you heard what they heard last, believe it or not. Some examples.

#1- Would you like to pick up your order, or would you like us to deliver it to your home?

#2- Would you like to put 50% down today, or would you prefer to pay the entire amount and get the 5% prepaid discount?

#3- Would you like to pay with check or credit card?

The McAddon Close- Did you know that when McDonald's first started asking, *"Would you like a Coke and fries with that?"* In the first 30 days they generated an additional 180 million dollars in sales. 180 million dollars in sales! It seems like this technique, which I call the McAddon Close, is all over the world now ... *Would you like a muffin with your coffee? Would you like dessert tonight? Would you like to purchase the extended warranty? Would you like me shampoo with your haircut today? Would you like some lottery tickets to go with your* *gas purchase today?* To you, this should mean that if you are not suggesting add-on sales with your orders, you are missing the boat!

Creating Raving Testimonials

Testimonials make the sales game much easier. When you say something about yourself it's bragging, but when somebody else says something about you it's proof! That is the bare-bones essence of a good testimonial. So, do you have a file folder with testimonials? Are you using them on a regular basis in your marketing, literature, website, and direct Mail pieces?

Conversion

The key to a successful sales system is conversion, turning prospects into customers. It's in your telephone skills, your presentation techniques, and your follow up procedures, so try these techniques out right away. The sooner you try what you have learned, the faster it will become part of your process.

CHAPTER 6

Pricing For Profit

There is an intimate relationship between the three different areas of your business that go into what I call the Power Triad: marketing, sales, and pricing. They each are interconnected with each other in such a way that it is impossible to attain a high level of success if any one of these three areas are weak, they are all connected at the hip. On that note, I would like to share something that has become very special to me over the years.

Ode to Pricing

It is unwise to pay too much, but it is worse to pay too little.

When you pay too much you lose a little money.

That is all.

When you pay too little, you sometimes lose everything because the thing that you bought was incapable of doing the thing that you bought it to do!

The common law of business balance prohibits pain a little and getting a lot.

It cannot be done...

And if you deal with the lowest bidder, it is well to add something for the risk that you run.

And if you do that, you will have enough to pay for something better period.

There is hardly anything in the world that someone cannot make a little worse and sell a little cheaper.

And the people, who consider price alone, are this man's lawful prey.

Believe it or not, this poem was written back in the 1800s by a man named John Ruskin, and it's as appropriate today as it was 220 years ago. My favorite line is, *"There is hardly anything in the world that someone cannot make a little worse comma and sell a little cheaper."*

The basic rule of supply and demand make something worth a higher price if that product is in demand. For example, I remember when the PT cruiser came out many years ago. My best friend had one on order for nearly six months because everybody wanted one. I would venture to say that he didn't get much of a discount, if any, on his purchase. There may have even been some dealerships that were charging more than a sticker price, because they could!

The other thing that allows you to charge more is that your customer wants the product emotionally. We have all heard the terrible stories of when people pay less for something, but it turns out to be a huge disaster. The price may have been right, but the true cost was very high.

The key comes down to whether we can create value for our clients, giving them something that has perceived value and benefits their life in some way. A classic example is in the auto business. You all have seen the television commercials from car dealers that say,

"Sunday, Sunday, Sunday noon until midnight! All cars must go! And we are prepared to sell you a car for a dollar over invoice hyphen no tricks, no gimmicks, no kidding!"

As a potential customer, that has very little to no value. At least very little perceived value. What happens after I drive the car home? What kind of service will I get?

I'd be more likely to buy if the commercial said, *"Our prices are $100 more than anybody else is, but our service is guaranteed to be 110% better than anybody else's service."*

Underneath that are pictures of their customers telling you why they paid an extra $100 and that the service is wonderful! They would probably grab a fair share of the market, don't you think?

Of course, not everyone will buy value; 30 to 40% of all people will buy based on price. That's the bad news. The good news is that 60 to 70% of all people will buy value if you provide it to them.

The Power Pricing Self-Test

Before we get too much farther, I want to clear the cobwebs out of your brain. We're going to start with the Power Pricing Self-Test and see where you are with your understanding of pricing strategy. This will take only about 5 minutes, so grab that pen and notepad, sit down in your favorite easy chair, and jot down some ideas as we go along.

Here we go.

A- How do you feel about your current price list?
B- Do you know your cost on each of your products and services?

If so, what are they?

C- Do you offer Ala carte pricing as well as packages or bundles? Whether you do or not, what were the factors that you considered when making your decision?

D- What is your markup factor, or how did you decide what to charge for each of your products and services?

E- How much does it cost you per month, per day, and even per hour to keep the doors open at your business, regardless of whether you have any business coming through your doors? This applies to both physical and virtual businesses.

F- Do you raise prices at least once a year to cover the additional expense of operating a business? If not, when was the last time you did change your pricing?

G- Could you raise your prices 5% next week and 5% in six months without giving your customers a heart attack?

H- Have you done a competitive analysis of other businesses in your niche to find out where they stand with their pricing structures? Where are you in the pricing hierarchy?

I- If you could create a life that had everything in it that your heart desires, what would it be? (you should already have this answer)

J- Do you feel your current pricing structure will allow you to get there someday?

K- What changes would have to be made for you to be able to attain your dreams and goals?

Many of these questions may require you to spend some time crunching numbers and doing some calculations. That's good! Make the time to get this accomplished as soon as possible- I would recommend today. There's no better time than right now to improve your business!

Addressing Pricing Issues

Your ability to handle pricing questions relies heavily on your belief in yourself, and your products and services. Before you can address price issues with your customers, you need to address it with yourself. If you don't have an unshakable faith that your products are worth the price, you will not be able to sell them. Your product and service maybe better than your competitors, but without the skills required to be able to price and sell your work, it will be for not.

THREE METHODS OF PRICING

There are basically three different methods that most businesses use in order to determine what the price should be for each of their products and services.

Cost-Based Pricing

Using this strategy, your pricing is based on what it costs you to produce a blue widget. This number is then multiplied by a factor in order to come up with the selling price. This multiplication factor must cover all the costs of running your business- your payroll, utilities, lease, cars, taxes, your compensation, and of course profit.

The 1st order of business is getting your arms around the cost of operating. You must have a complete grasp of these numbers in order to be the best businessperson you can be and price your work blue widget accordingly. The first expense category is your capital expenses or your investment costs. Things like real estate, vehicles, equipment that you purchase, furniture, etc.

The second category contains your general expenses, like your pay and benefits, employee pay and benefits, lease payments, electric, phone, trash, insurance, taxes, advertising, education, bookkeeping services, etc. These things must be paid every month, whether you have any business or not.

The third category consists of your cost of sales (COS). This is what it costs you to produce a blue widget from beginning to end. This can be tricky. If I were to ask you what it costs your business to produce a single blue widget, ready for delivery, what would you say? You can't simply say, well, my supplier charges me $2, so if I sell it, I'm making an $8.00 profit! It doesn't quite work that way. Let's think about this question for a minute.

In addition to the supplier bill, there was the time that you spent talking with the customer on the phone, putting their order together or planning their service. If you have salespeople, there are commissions to be paid, prepping charges, packaging, service technicians to be paid, and ultimately the delivery of said product or service. If you don't know what your COS are for every one of your products and/or services, I want you to spend some time with your nose in your books to come up with numbers.

So, if the COS accounts for only a small percentage of the actual price, where does the rest of the money go? Well, after the COS is subtracted from the selling price, that leaves you with what we call the margin contribution or gross profit. That is the amount that is used to pay the overhead. Whatever is leftover being of course, your profit.

So how do you determine the right selling price? Great question! Once you do a competitive analysis, evaluate your lifestyle goals, and determine what is best for your business, you will come up with the answers, guaranteed!

Competitive-Based Pricing

Unlike cost-based pricing, competition-based pricing considers what your competitors are doing with their pricing strategies. As you are very aware, some products and services are more price sensitive than others, so you must be aware of what is going on in your marketplace. I'm going to ask you the price of some everyday items and I want you to come up with an answer period ready?

A gallon of milk

A pack of gum

A gallon of gas

A new digital camera

A can of pumpkin pie filling

A soda

A movie ticket

A car wash

A Japanese Dwarf Maple tree

An all you can eat buffet

A gallon of bleach

A drive-thru combo meal

A pound of Morel mushrooms

A nice bottle of wine on Friday night

A hanging plant basket

A desktop computer

A Lamborghini sports car

A box of facial tissue

A ream printing paper

An electric dog fence

Most of these items probably assigned a value instantly in your brain. Other items- like a can of pumpkin pie filling or Japanese Maple, or a Lamborghini, or the electric dog fence- may have stumped you just a bit.

If you were to go into five different grocery stores to compare the price of a gallon of milk, they would all be within a tight range. You probably wouldn't find one store that charged a dollar and another that charged $10, would you? Same with a gallon of gas, or a car wash, for anything that is considered a commodity.

The prices must be perceived as at least being in the ballpark or, as consumers, we close our minds. If the local gas station was charging $45.00 for a gallon of gas, would we even think about stopping in? I don't think so.

What items in your industry are considered commodities or need to be at least perceived as being in the ballpark for competitive reasons? In looking at your pricing from a competitive standpoint, you need to be aware of what your potential customers will gauge your worthiness on- how they will determine whether you are in the ballpark. So, wouldn't it make sense to make sure that your pricing, or at least the perception of your pricing, was viewed as being competitive?

You may actually be the most expensive in town because of all the little things you do to add perceived value and to provide your customer with a luxury experience, but the way your pricing is presented must still show your customers that you are in the ballpark.

Publishing Prices on Your Website

This is a great question, regardless of the industry that you are in! My view of websites is that they should exist to create excitement and entice a prospect to either send you an email, or better yet, pick up the phone and give you a call. The job of your website is not strictly to sell, which is what you are doing when you post your prices on the Internet. If you are going to do that, you had better make sure you are doing a great job of creating value for whatever it is you are selling.

A website can build a relationship a website can't build a relationship, create a report, or even ask questions. That all must be done by human by the human element. However, the sales process can be made easier by professionally designed website that has good content and helps educate the customer and prospect.

Now, if you would like to post ranges, that is perfectly fine, but remember that you don't want your website to be your only salesperson. It should not decide who gets in and who doesn't. That should be up to you or someone on your staff. Now, if you strictly offered digital products and your website is your storefront, then this doesn't necessarily apply to you, but it is still vitally important that you build value with everything that you do.

Lifestyle or Demand-Based Pricing

This is perhaps the most important element to consider when determining what prices you charge. It's a combination of everything you have ever done to create a high perceived value for your products and services with the lifestyle you want for yourself and your family.

All these things must be determined before you can decide on what price to charge, since the money that you bring in is directly related to what dreams you have in your life.

So, how much will your market bear? Unfortunately, I don't know that answer. That's something only you can determine.

What's best?

Have you been able to figure out which method would be best for your business? Hopefully you realize that the best method to use is a combination of the three.

First, figure out what it cost you to open your doors in the morning, what it costs you to produce your products and services, and then assign a markup factor to come up with a price for each product. This is the absolute lowest that your pricing can be comma and let you plan on losing money and not being around in the year to answer your phones...

Then, do a competitive analysis to see where you are compared to the other players in your market. Finally, determine what kind of demand there is for your products and services and what lifestyle choices you have made for yourself and your family. Put all three sets of data together and you will be able to come up with a pricing structure that is both profitable and well thought out.

In previous chapters, we looked extensively at how to create value for your products and services, how to position those products in the mind of your perfect customer, how to build a positive image in your community comma and how to create a sales atmosphere that compels customers to spend more money with you. All these things must go into your calculations as well. The goal is to create a high level of desire long before you ever talk about price. It's like building a house- the foundation must be poured before you put up your large big screen TV in the living room!

A reminder that marketing, selling, and pricing are all connected at the hip and create the Power Triad.

Will your method of doing business appeal to everybody? Of course not! Are there people in the world who will always be looking for ways to get things on the cheap? You bet! They are the kinds of people who will go to Walmart and by their own oil filter, then drive all the way across town to go to another store to buy the oil because it's on sale.

Then, convinced they have saved Seven whole dollars, happily crawl under the car to change the oil and filter themselves. This person may get their oil change for less, but they'll spend 3 hours doing it. The price may have been right, but the cost was very high indeed.

"Cheap things are not good and good things are not cheap"

THE MYTHS AND REALITIES OF PRICING

Do you believe in the Loch Ness Monster? What about Bigfoot? Or UFO's? Or how about this one: you can eat everything you want, as much as you want, and still lose weight? These are some hefty myths that have been perpetuated for quite some time- and it seems as though there will always be a group of people who will buy into them. Well, there are also some pricing myths that I would like to dispel once and for all.

Myth #1: People Buy Because Of Price

Wrong! If you insist on selling based on price, your customers will buy because of price. Sure, price is important, but it doesn't have to be as important as a lot of other factors- that is, unless you believe in this price Smith. There have been many businesses over the years, and price usually comes in 5th as far as the reason that people make their purchasing decisions. Other factors like quality, experience, level of service, and referral usually place higher than price on the importance scale.

Myth #2: Lower is Better

Let's talk in broad terms about the impediment of discounting. Let's imagine there are 100 units of a product that you sell in your business. If you give a 10% discount on these, you will need to sell 111 additional units to make the same amount of money as selling 100 at full price. At a 15% discount, you would need to sell 118 units. You'll have to do more work to earn the same amount and you make less, on a percentage basis, because you have more time and overhead invested.

On the other hand, if you add 10% to your prices, which you

should be doing once a year anyway, you only must sell 91 units to generate the same revenues. At 15% and you're down to just 87 units.

The point is that your customers may not be as price sensitive as you fear they are. They may tolerate a price increase much better than you think. Additionally, they may not even respond to a decrease in price as enthusiastically as you need them two for that decrease to be profitable for you.

Myth #3- Price is What Matters

When we think about how to price our products and services, we assume that our focus should be on the price. But there are many other factors that go into determining profits and cash flow, as I have mentioned. Price will only matter if you allow it to matter. Don't fall into this deathtrap! You need to charge what you think you are worth.

An increase in price will increase a prospects perception of you; It decrease in price will decrease the perceived value. Many people assume that price equates to quality which means they won't buy your products in less your price is high enough. You may remember the story about a riding lawn mower that I tried to sell several years ago. In my initial ad, I set the price so low that people figured there must have been something wrong with it. As a result, I didn't get a single call. When I raised the price to $200, I sold it instantly!

Factors That Really Do Effect Pricing

There are several major factors that will affect your ability to have a successful pricing strategy in today's competitive marketplace. These include the branding and marketing that you're currently doing or not doing, having a highly defined sale system that begins the very first second someone is exposed to your business and continues long after your customers do business with you , having a complete understanding of your competitors strengths and weaknesses, and having an unequivocal belief in yourself and your ability as a modern day entrepreneur.

Price is where you get what is yours, where all those wonderful things you do for your customers are supposed to be reciprocated. When it comes to pricing you must be sure that you are getting what you deserve- and nobody will pay you more than what you asked for, so be careful not to underprice yourself.

So, how can you tell if you have poor pricing? If you constantly find yourself having to explain your price list, or if the prices always seems to be an issue, or if you are always changing your prices, or- here's the big one- you always seem to be busy but don't have anything to show for it ... Those are all bad signs. If this is the case, it sounds like you it may be time for a price list makeover!

Something that will help you with some of these issues is to work on your image through marketing materials, refining your sales skills and techniques, and most importantly by putting more emphasis on building relationships with your customers. This will lead to a decrease of price sensitivity all by itself. The stronger your relationship with your customer, the less important price becomes. This is the magic carpet that will take you to where you want to be.

Learn to answer the pricing questions confidently and professionally. If you educate your customers, price is rarely an issue.

Building an Effective Price List

What does your price list alone communicate about the value in your business? Is your pricing clear, concise, and easy to understand? When someone looks at your pricing, does it make their head explode with confusion?

There are some simple to implement techniques that will help to make your price list a much more effective sales tool hyphen and that will, intern, increase your sales averages substantially

Research Other Businesses in Your Market

You don't need to reinvent the wheel. There are plenty of great price lists already on the market in your industry, you just need to get your hands on them. It may be as simple as going to their website, or even calling them and suggesting that you have a cup of coffee together.

Here's a novel idea: call all your competitors in your market, or if you are a virtual business you can connect people via Zoom or Skype and have a Mastermind session. Have everyone bring their price list, some marketing materials, and a business card. There isn't really any secret way of making money in your industry. The more you can share with your competition, the more they will share with you. In the end, you are all trying to accomplish the same goal, and if you can increase a customer's awareness, everyone will do better.

The purpose of this is not so you can copy the prices, but rather so you can get ideas for graphic design, layout, creative ways to bundle products and services together, or unique items that you can offer your customers. It's all part of the creative process.

Find the Best Paper Money Can Buy

The paper that your price list is printed on speaks volumes about the quality of and value that you provide, so don't cut corners with this part of your business. Once you have made that initial impression on someone, it's virtually impossible to change it, so do it right from the beginning. Go down to your local print shop and ask to see their best line of paper. It really doesn't matter what industry you are in; your pricing should be presented as professionally as possible.

Keep Your Ala Carte Pricing High

This will create value for your packages, bundles, or collections. We will talk about how to build package is a little later on, but putting a group of products together for your customers to purchase is a very good thing, after all, the more decisions you ask your customers to make during the sales process, the more difficult it will be at the end when it comes time for the most important the most important decision, which is how much to spend are they going to spend. The easier you can make it on your customer, the higher your sales averages will be and the happier they will be.

Feature A "Most Popular" & A "Best Value" Package

The reason for this is very simple. Human nature says that people like to belong to a group and feel safe when they know that others are doing the same thing. Even if you don't have a "Most Popular" package, make one up!

Before long, it will become your most popular simply via the power of suggestion. Obviously, the package with the highest price will also be the one that has the best value because of all the savings that have been built in. Make sure to point out this fact right on your price list. If they believe in it, they will buy it!

How do you determine which package should be your most popular? Here's a cool little technique. Once you have determined what your averages are for each type of product and service you offer, your most popular package should be at the level that is higher than your current average.

For example, let's say you have an average of $200 on one of your most popular products. I would recommend having your most popular package between $250-$350. Then, everything you do should be with that package in mind. This will bring your average is up by nearly 20% and will give your customer a great value at the same time. If your averages are higher or lower than this, you will have to adjust accordingly, but I think you understand the concept.

Have A "Whopper Package" In Your Price List

What is a whopper package you ask? It's something that appears to be so incredibly expensive that nobody in their right mind would ever invest in it. It's a package that has everything, including the kitchen sink. The purpose of a whopper? To make the other packages look and feel better. It's only there to create value for the other packages. A little later there will be an exercise that will help you generate some ideas on what you can include in a whopper package.

Never Discount Your Prices

When you discount your prices, you lower the perceived, which can have a long-term effect on your ability to charge what you are worth. Giving something away for free is always better than giving somebody a discount. Add value but try not to discount!

Pricing Strategies

When I go to one of the big retail malls in my area, there are a few stores that I love to visit. One is Bath & Body Works, because it seems they always have some incredible deals on their product's- and the deal is always the same. For many years it was buy three get one free. Even if you plan on only purchasing a single item when you went in, you really couldn't get out of there without stepping up and buying two more so you can get the 4th and no charge.

In fact, 84% of their customers end up purchasing three to get one free. Isn't that incredible? The last time I was in there, the deal had been changed to buy 2 get one free, and I bet this strategy will even be more successful!

Victoria's Secret is another store that does an incredible job of packaging and bundling. A few of years ago I took one of my workshop classes to the mall so they could see how the big boys do things, and we stood there and witnessed a magical moment. A woman had taken a pair of panties up to the cash register to purchase. She was greeted by a friendly sales associate who enthusiastically supported the lady's choice of style and color. She then said the following, *"If you purchase one pair, they are $7.00, or you can get five pairs for only $5 each."*

The lady almost jumped out of her dress as she quickly rushed to select four more pairs so she can get them for only $5 each when she was ready to check out the sales associate then said, *"If you like to open a Victoria's Secret charge account today, I can give you 90 days to make your first Payment, no interest for a year , plus give you a $25 gift card. Are you interested in signing up today?*

Well by now, the lady thought she had won the lottery and happily filled out the application, received her $25 gift card, and went back into the aisles to pick up several other items. By the time she was done she had spent over $200 and walked out as happy as a spring chicken. She had originally planned on spending $7!

The same dynamic happens when you are at the airport terminal and want to buy a pair of sunglasses. You can buy one pair for $14.00, or two pairs for $20. It works, or they wouldn't do it!

It just goes to show, you can make people buy what you want them to buy if you can make the alternative unattractive! This, my friend, is exactly why you should offer packages in addition to your Ala Carte pricing.

Designing Irresistible Packages

Packages appeal to customers because they reduce the number of ordering decisions needed and offer a good value. They can also boost your bottom line by giving the customer a strong incentive to spend a little, or a lot, more. But how do you create packages that are irresistible? Let's do an exercise and generate some ideas. We'll start with some brainstorming, then talk about ways to implement these ideas into your product mix.

For these examples, let's visit our friends at John Doe's Photography Studios. Regardless of what industry you are in, these techniques can also be applied. You will just have to come up with your own list of items to include. Once you understand the concept, it becomes much easier to apply to your own business.

Adding Benefits

What are some things that you could offer your customers that would be so irresistible that people would have to be fools not to respond? I want you to remove all obstacles and allow your mind to wander just a bit, OK? Don't worry about cost, or price, or anything like that for now. We will get to that soon enough. For now, just let your mind create. What would compel a potential customer to want to do business with you instead of anybody else in your market? Here are just a few ideas to get you started.

#1- A complimentary limousine rental when someone books one of your premiere packages.

#2- A day at the spa for a bride, and perhaps the bridesmaids 2, maybe even mom and grandma. You could include a massage, a facial, manicure, or pedicure!

#3- A complimentary night for two at the finest local resort, including dinner and champagne.

#4 A 2-volume album set for the bride and groom, an album for mom and dad, and a nice album for grandma.

#5- Unlimited time not just on the wedding day, but on Friday night at the rehearsal dinner, and Sunday morning when they are opening their gifts in front of friends and family members.

#6- A hot air balloon ride complete with a champagne breakfast.

#7- Unlimited gift wallets for all guests to send with their thank you cards.

#8- A signature mat for all the guests to sign at the reception.

#9- Thank you cards for every single guest, with envelopes and postage.

#10- A DVD slide show of all their images- not just for the bride and groom, but for mom and dad, the grandparent's, and the wedding party.

In a perfect world, your Whopper Package- your top of the line, fantasy package- would include all these items, right? How much would it cost for you to build a package that included everything on this list? I'll tell you one thing: it won't be cheap! But it will show your customer what can be done, if money isn't an issue. The Whopper Package will also make all your other packages look much less intimidating in comparison, and probably encourage a large enough purchase to get at least some of the whopper perks.

Now, as the bride is hearing about all these wonderful things that are included in this premium collection, her mind is taking "ownership" of each one of them. Remember, the bride has been dreaming about this day since she was 5 years old! If you have done this correctly; the bride and groom will take complete ownership of the vision that you are painting with this package.

When selling, you should always start with this top dollar package, then work your way down the list. This is called "takeaway selling", because you are taking things away to create something more affordable. Because it appeals to the emotions, that sense of wanting in our clients, it can be extremely effective if done properly. If you have been married at some point in your life you know that emotions drive how much money you spent on things simply because you wanted to. It may not make sense to spend $25,000 on a handwoven bridal dress flown in from Italy, but by golly the bride wanted it!

Once you have described in detail what is entailed in your whopper package (which is the "Best Value"), the bride will want everything you have included. Then next package down is called the "drop" since you are not only dropping the price, you are also dropping several items that the bride and groom have already imagined having in their package. As a result, when you drop down to the next package that doesn't include the romantic getaway, or the balloon ride, or albums for grandparents... Well, it almost feels like she is giving up something that she already bought. And the next collection down includes even fewer items that she has decided she just absolutely must have if she is to have the perfect wedding. This package can be called your most popular.

So, what does the smallest package include? Not much. For a package or bundling strategy to work, there must be a reason for a customer to go up into the next larger package. If you give them everything they want in the smallest package, there is no incentive for them to invest more get the point?

This technique can work in just about any industry…a retail store, online store, wholesaler, manufacturer, digital products, consulting, landscaping, car wash, accounting firm, and more. The above techniques will work like magic!

Stand Out from The Crowd

The fun part is sitting down to come up with what your different packages include and what you can do to create irresistible offers.

Here are some generic ideas on things that you can include for your customers-

#1- A coffee gift card for all new customers that come into you during the month of February.

#2- A movie pass for the entire family.

#3- Free oil changes for year with minimum purchase.

#4- A free stuffed animal from a local children's store for all new customers during the month of December.

#5- A gift card to their favorite store.

#6- A free cart of groceries from a local grocery store with minimum purchase.

#9- You pick!

Any of these items can be used as an incentive to get your customers to come to you in the 1st place, or enticements to get them to step up to the next package. If Mrs. Jones sees that the difference between package A and package B is $200, but she receives an additional $350.00 a value... Well, what do you think she's likely to do? If your price list has built-in incentives an enticements, it will become your #1 salesperson, which can take some pressure off you. Wouldn't that be nice?

CHAPTER 7

Harnessing social media

The Elephant in the Room

Can we talk?

First and foremost, I want to say I'm a firm believer in the power of social media (SM). If we're smart, we use SM tools to our advantage. Today, business owners are facing an increasing demand on their time from a myriad of sources. The market has told us that we must become regular contributors to every SM platform or be left behind to rot.

The world must know what we're doing on a continuous basis or customers won't support our products and services, preferring to buy from others with more splashy SM banners and more active profiles. While it's true that SM has given us tons of possible tools to help grow revenue, it is by no means is the end all, be all.

I am addicted to knowledge. The Internet gives me access to everything I could ever want to know and then some about any topic I can imagine. Articles, videos, blogs, online courses, sports scores, webinars, educational websites, and a never-ending smorgasbord of stuff that is made to enrich our lives in one form or another.

What an amazing global marketplace for the UE to explore. My kids can learn about the history of Pompeii, how to build a Pinewood Derby car, find out about the Monarch butterfly, or dive deep into the history of the island of Aruba- all with the touch of their fingertips.

But there is something happening right before our very eyes. By the time we realize it, our businesses may be in real jeopardy of failure.

Listen. Do you hear that? It's the sound of your time being sucked right out from underneath you. You have voluntarily traded your attention and time for a small amount of gratification that may or may not have anything to do with your ultimate goals. You have freely given of our most precious resource, your time, in exchange for an adrenaline rush for a millisecond, when your face is buried in our device.

On average, we check our emails one hundred and fifty times a day, and there are two billion people who spend fifty minutes a day or more on Facebook and Instagram. That doesn't even include time spent watching YouTube videos of cat tricks, creating silly videos on Snapchat, or tweeting a picture of what they ate for dinner.

Using SM provides us with immediate rewards for very little effort, and your brain begins to desire more stimulation. It's a vicious circle of doom. For me, I prefer to utilize my limited bandwidth for more productive activities.

If you spend an average of only 1 hour a day surfing around (and that number is very light indeed), that 1 hour of time that had to come from somewhere else. You don't get a 25th hour of your day. Something had to give…

You can create the perfect lifestyle for you and your family and build the most fantastic business in the world, only to have it all fall apart because you don't have the self-discipline to say no to the call of the Internet siren. Just because somebody or something asks for your time doesn't mean you need to give it up so easily!

All SM platforms were created with a single mission: to make money! They have done this by creating communities of fans, and by selling that attention to sponsors for cash. They deliver value to us, the customer, and that value has a price tag on it in the form of various ads.

I admit that trying to control your online habits is a bit like fighting a Hydra, but you need to control your urges if you want to realize your maximum potential.

Many of you may be yelling at me right now. That's okay. I can take it. With that said, I only want the best for every single businessperson who has a dream and is willing to risk making those dreams come true.

There are many other resources out there that teach you how to utilize the Internet in appropriate ways, but here are some tips and tricks that may help you resist the urge to stay up until midnight browsing Facebook:

1. Give yourself an hour in the morning before looking at your device or logging on to your computer. Your device will be waiting for you, I promise.
2. Create device-free zones in your house. You can talk to your spouse and children without them checking their text messages every 45 seconds.
3. Set up a block of time (POD) during your day when you can respond to these demands on your time. If you set aside some time for the Internet, it will prevent you from being sidetracked during the time you're focused on other projects.

The bottom line is this- To build the lifestyle of your dreams in productive alignment with the business of your dreams, you will need to master your control over the use of the Internet. It's that simple.

I believe we all have become victims, but it's not too late to take back control of our time and reinvest it into creating your perfect lifestyle!

Now, let's get back to business…

"Effective use of social media marketing raises brand awareness and increases conversion rates by 50%"

The question is, how do you achieve such a brutal efficiency? By understanding the nature of social media and key factors of a successful SM campaign we'll explain in this chapter.

Today, different social media channels are used to collect millions of free dollars in direct startup funding from everyday people. Social networks are also the vital sales channels that, when used in an optimal way, drive conversion rates through the roof.

However, the primary role of social media is having an open communication channel with your people. That's what should be your ONLY goal and strategy when designing a customized approach to a specific SM network.

"Leads and sales come as the result of a warm and intimate connection between your brand and its fans"

All this to say: you shouldn't force the sales but instead, let them happen naturally, as a part of the evolving process of building a community.

Therefore, the purpose of your SM activities is lead generation.

Lead generation in the digital environment equals the situation where, in an analog world, I'm opening the door and inviting you in after talking to you on the phone a few days earlier. Something MLMs and high-ticket affiliates used to do back in the day, and what some of them are still practicing. Only, today, they are more prone to using social networks than calling you on the phone.

As with everything in life, there are those who are doing it right and there are also those who are dead wrong in their approach to social media marketing.

LESSON 1: The Things You Think You Know but You Don't

Social media is a one-of-a-kind beast that regularly makes entrepreneurs go crazy because of its apparent complexity. There's nothing in our everyday lives that resembles the behavior of social networks and the users that drive that behavior. And that's the common mistake people do when designing SM strategies.

Even Facebook, where we are posting under our real names, doesn't reflect our usual behavior.

Therefore, if you are creating a campaign and your premise is an analog human behavior, the results will be disappointing, to say the least. Here's a little demonstration of the key behavioral difference between the analog and digital worlds.

Say that you are in a café, early in the morning, sipping a coffee and scrolling the paper. Obviously, you are not in a hurry. You are taking the time to go through all those columns and articles. Perhaps you'll even order another coffee because there's so much in the newspaper.

All that time, what you are doing, is dwelling on the same media channel, reading whole articles for over an hour and possibly even longer.

Once you come home and turn on your laptop, your behavior suddenly changes. You'll briefly skim through titles, moving quickly from one media channel to another. You'll repeat the same pattern across the social networks you'll visit.

For some strange reason, once we are online, we are always in the hurry. But when we sit down in a cafe or a bar or in the middle of the field, we are taking our time. In fact, there are situations—and I'll let you assume the one I'm referring to—when you'll even read the fine print on a fabric softener container. The real kicker is that you'll feel enthusiastic about it. However, you won't even bother reading past the title let alone clicking on the link placed within the body of an article.

For that to happen, there must be something truly extraordinary in that title and in each following paragraph. At the same time, a less powerful title in a newspaper will make you read the entire article and even follow recommendations if any.

Imagine how difficult it is to maintain the level of the utmost excellence in crafting social posts to not only build and retain the current base of followers but to make those people call others in.

However, if you follow a few simple rules, the results may surprise you.

QUIZ: A Page or A Group?

Facebook is still the undisputed king of social networks. And for brands and businesses, Facebook is offering two options: a page or a group.

In your opinion, which option returns better results?

A) Page
B) Group

A tribe will always outperform a team. Therefore, the correct answer is B) A group. Because creating a page is nothing but listing things as you'd do in the yellow pages. Creating a group, on the other hand, means building a community.

This is where basic human behavior kicks in. When we feel a part of a larger group, we are devoting ourselves to it. We will defend it, work in its best interest, invest time and money into its future well-being – without even considering our best interests. In other words, we will gladly sacrifice for the benefits of the community because its success is our success.

A page simply doesn't hold that kind of power. In our minds, the page is yet another dull listing of meaningless posts and offerings coming from someone who's only interested in squeezing money out of our pockets. And then I go to one of my chosen groups and spend a juicy amount of money on a thing I don't even need. It's a paradox but, at least, we are aware of it.

Two exact same posts- One published on the page- The other published in the group. The difference in conversion rates is simply mind-blowing. Provided, of course, that we are running an active community.

For now, let's just say that a group creates a far greater trust currency value due to our sense of belonging. I simply trust my fellow tribesman, that's all.

But regardless of how powerful Facebook still is, it is far from being the "one-size-fits-all" type of social media. Some profitable demographics congregate on perhaps less famous social networks and if you miss them, that will have a devastating effect on your overall efforts.

LESSON 2: Choosing the Right Media

The key here is K-Y-C or Know Your Customer. From there, we are building a list of potential social media where our customer not only spends most of the time but also where he or she feels most comfortable. And that's the key right there.

Just like a group creates a more powerful effect than a page, in the same fashion, specific social media is perceived in a more intimate way than any other. Sure, Tom is visiting an array of social networks but in his core, he is a Redditor. That's where he feels he belongs. That's where his people are. And he is extremely defensive when it comes to Reddit. It goes so far that he will spit fire across Subreddits when he spots a shameless plug so lamely "disguised" as a Reddit post. The same will happen to ads that are created by someone who doesn't understand the specific nature of that particular social media.

What's the key takeaway here?

Know Your Environment

Or, at least, hire someone who's deeply connected to it. And almost every other social network beyond Facebook, WhatsApp, and Instagram means going alternative and niching down. These three mainstream social channels are a free-for-all but with networks like Reddit, Quora, Snapchat, and many other alternative channels, you must tread carefully.

"The SN is, therefore, chosen by having our primary goals in mind"

So, what are we truly trying to achieve with our engagement in social media marketing?

To build a tribe across the digital universe by targeting social media that best fit our brand's long-term interests.

How Do We Choose the Best Fit? By…

- Researching the habits of our targeted demographic.
- Forward-thinking.

As a rule of thumb, every ten to twelve years, brands are rejuvenating their base of followers. For example, some of them are dipping into the pool of teenagers on social media such as Snapchat by adjusting their messages so once these young boys and girls grow older, they would instinctively become customers. Others are targeting the working class that will soon retire. Realtors are regularly hanging around students to build a long-lasting connection. Sooner or later, these men and women will start generating income and guess who will be the first realtor they will call?

In other words, while we are building strategies for our most immediate demographic, we must think into the future and communicate our brand to a demographic that has yet to join our base of customers. That's the main premise of high-voltage branding anyway – the long-term thinking and planning. Remember, a cult-level fan base has a far stronger bond with a brand than just another group of followers.

How Do We Conduct Research?

The best thing about the Internet is that it has quickly produced bloggers that blog about blogging, about blogging, about blogging. Therefore, a simple search term like *"list of social networks with descriptions"* will return a plethora of results. All you must do is to extract the most valuable information from each article.

Social media	**Predominant age group**	**Predominant gender**	**Best suited for**
FACEBOOK	22+	males and females	all interests and industries, suckers for causes
INSTAGRAM	16-30	males and females	beauty, fashion, fashion accessories, gadgets, travel
REDDIT	16-30	predominantly males but with a substantial female base	cool innovations, alternative, out-of-the-box ideas, tech stuff, blockchain
SNAPCHAT	teenagers	males and females	best for rejuvenating and/or building a future customer base
TWITTER	16-45	males and females	all industries and interests but with the emphasis on trendy and innovative ideas
PINTEREST	16-45	males and females	design and travel

This is, of course, generalization based on the capital interests of the dominant corpus within a specific social network. That's not to say that you cannot sell an aging cream on Twitter!

But how often should you post? Can you push it over the limit or, on the other hand, be too silent?

LESSON 3- Maintaining the Optimal Balance

"As the rule of thumb, 3 posts per week are the sweet spot"

However, that's highly subjective and individual. For example, if your marketing strategy is serving regular news, then this doesn't apply. But if you are an affiliate marketer, infopreneur or a traditional brick and mortar entrepreneur, regardless of your niche or industry, stay within these boundaries.

To this, another rule applies:

"If you don't have anything smart to say, skip it"

As we said, our behavior online can be best described as a spoiled brat whose impatience is only measured by its megalomaniac tendencies and impossible expectations. So, keep it simple, dynamic, and interesting.

That is to say that, you should mix it up and always strive to provide a visual experience over the textual one. Even infopreneurs must obey this rule because social media is just a communication channel. It's the bus stop where you are picking your passengers and taking them to their destination, which can be either a web location or your analog store.

But even a visual post almost exclusively contains a little piece of text. Especially so-called, lead and money magnets.

EXERCISE- Writing A Perfect SM Post

This is the most important element of your post. Even in articles, you can have a 3000-word piece, filled with the expensive infographics and videos, but without a great headline, no one will even notice it.

Crafting Headlines Is Almost A Science

Crafting a great headline is harder than writing the content itself.

In other words, the conversion of your post largely depends on the effectiveness of the headline.

Nielsen provides a great HINT by pointing to the masters of the headlines.

Visit the BBS News website and notice the headlines. Everything is said in five words.

5 Key Elements of Every Good Headline

According to Jacob Nielsen, founder of the NNGroup:

- It must be short
- Has the ability to summarize the entire article
- Most important keywords (hooks) are in the first two words
- Must be understandable on its own
- Must be predictable

To be most effective, your headline should be no more than 6 words

The absolute importance of a great headline can be further seen in the next rule.

"RULE #2: Your content has to trigger the emotional switch or it will fail"

"*What's in it for me*?"

This is the basic question and the answer has a direct impact on the reader's decision to:

1. Click through or
2. Skip it altogether

You want these emotional switches:

- Joy
- Fear
- Excitement
- Rage
- Love
- Curiosity

Any of the listed works. If your post is not able to intrigue the reader by provoking at least some emotional reaction, don't even bother.

Your objective is to attempt to predict what emotion will be evoked from your post.

That means that if you know what motivates your crowd, you can adjust the post in the most optimal way. As a result, your conversion rates will soar.

To figure this out, I recommend you spent some time browsing the Internet looking at attractive ads and posts. That's the best way to see what might possibly work for you in your industry. Still, since this is an ever-evolving environment, things can become boring and old overnight.

Just follow the two rules we explained earlier and once you've written a post, ask yourself this- Would I click on this?

Or even better- Is this beneficiary or damaging to my efforts in building a cult-level fan base?

Remember, the key purpose of social media marketing is not selling. It's building a tribe. So, when crafting your posts, keep in mind that your crowd responds to a very specific style and tone you set right from the start. Therefore, do not deviate from it.

Which headline motivates you more?

MIND WHAT YOU'RE DRINKING

vs.

DO YOU KNOW WHAT ARE YOU DRINKING?

Yes, we are using our premium bottled water as an example. What do you think would resonate better with our future bottled water cult?

The first one sounds instructional. Humans, in general, don't really respond well to instructions. But we are easily intrigued, regardless of our status. So, the second headline would probably return a far better conversion rate.

This is something you should always keep in mind when formulating your post's headline. Does it intrigue or trigger a certain level of revolt and discontent that might backfire?

"When in doubt, switch the roles. In other words, imagine yourself reading it. How would you react?"

CHAPTER 8

It's "GO TIME"

Hitting the launch button on anything new is a scary thing, but can introduce you to entire new worlds if you have the gumption to try.

However…

There is nothing truly unknown anymore. Running a business today is like finding a job a hundred years ago. The same set of challenges. The same anxiety. Those people were leaving their villages where they were able to provide for themselves and headed into the unknown; into these big and scary cities, none of them had a chance to explore prior to making the decision. There, only money could bring food on the table. The alternative was giving up and returning to poverty and borderline famine.

Luckily for us today, these brave men and women ignored their primordial fears and made that decisive leap that ultimately created the world we know.

Therefore, the only thing standing between you and business success is inherited laziness and the fear of failure.

You share both with every single human being on this planet. There's no such thing as being predisposed for success because success isn't given. It's a result of planned and executed series of steps that lead to the ultimate goal, which is absolute freedom.

The only way to reach that goal is to become an entrepreneur. Are there any guarantees?

Yes. Contrary to general consensus and like a gazillion blogs and books that paint the picture of uncertainty, the success is guaranteed if you invest yourself into it.

After all, we are talking about offering your products or services to a 4-billion people strong market. Half of them are shopping online which makes it incredibly easy to connect with them.

Today, more than ever before throughout our history, it has become increasingly easy to start and run your own show because unlike back then, this massive market is well within your reach. You don't even have to leave your home in some instances. There's this rising corpus of the new-age entrepreneurs who are making their money in their pajamas. We are talking about online entrepreneurs and freelance service providers who are rewriting the employment paradigm as we speak. Because for them, the work is not where you go anymore but what you do.

And without exceptions, they are considered entrepreneurs because they are in total control of their market, time and income. Just like you can be if you decide to take that simple leap of faith.

The best part about it is that you don't have to have faith in someone's ability to keep the company running so you'd receive your paycheck. The only person you got to have faith in is YOU and you alone. Admit it; it is easier to believe in yourself than to willingly put your life and your future in someone else's hands, isn't it?

So, what is the very first step to the new 24/7 paradigm? Export everything–and I mean everything–that's now swirling in your mind on the paper to visualize it. Don't even bother with some order of things. Just let it out as it's coming.

That's the moment when a daydream starts transforming into a new reality because it's not just a wave anymore but has a tangible physical shape.

How Are You Spending Your Dash?

Can you tell me what the following numbers are?

1825-1877

1776-1851

1962- 2003

They are life spans. There's a born-on date and a dead-on date. We have little control over either one of those events, but what we do have control over is what we do with the time in-between. It's called the "dash." It's everything that happens from the second you were born to the moment you die. It's your entire life boiled down into a minuscule hyphen!

The question I'd like you to marinate in your mind is: How are you spending your dash?

The dash is all you have to leave behind when you are done with your time on Earth. Are you making a difference in the lives of people who mean the most to you?

Now that you are done reading this book, I hope you have gained a renewed perspective on what's important in your life. Living the life of a UE means much more than running a successful business, it means living a life of meaning and purpose as well.

Another way of describing the in-between segment of your life is the gap. Here's where you are, there's where you want to be, and then there's the gap in between. We need to learn to love the gap because that's where most of our life is lived. Gap Thinking will help you understand the importance of your dash.

We all want to be better dads, moms, friends, bosses, and workers. We want to live a life that is rewarding and fulfilling, yet success and happiness seems to elude many people. Many people are mired in jobs they hate, marriages that are broken, and other quagmires. We all need something to strive for, work towards, and dream about.

What's your reason for getting out of bed every day? If you can't come up with a better reason than "I have to," then it's time to take a hard look at your life from 40,000 feet.

If you were to ask a group of elderly people what they would do differently if they could live their life all over again, I venture to say that 95 percent would answer that they would reflect more, risk more, and do more things that would live on after they were gone. The best part is that we don't have to wait until our life is nearly over before we can begin to live like this. You can begin today.

There's nothing sadder to me than when someone doesn't give his or her life enough value, or when someone says:

"I didn't live my life like I should have. I didn't achieve, I didn't take any risks." There's no going back to the beginning of the race.

When you go to sleep every night, it's one less day you have. Can you imagine getting up, going to work, and having to do things you don't like to do or are not very good at? That's not the kind of thing that makes you get up every day with a spring in your step.

But when you get up with a sense of purpose and you love what you do, it's going to bring your focus into a very narrow beam of high intensity energy bursting with very palpable results.

What's holding you back from living the life of your dreams? What steps can you take today to make those dreams come true? I've noticed many people do not have a real sense of direction, almost as if they were waiting for someone to show them the way. You must make the choice to move forward with your life and not sit around waiting for the magic to happen from out of the blue.

There are two kinds of people in this world: Those who wait for something to happen, and those who take the initiative and make things happen. If you need to change, don't make any more excuses.

Hoping that things will change has no effect. Only tangible actions on your part will make the difference!

Life is a very delicate balance. The challenge is to keep your perspective and discover or rediscover what's important to you. We never know when our time is up. Most people live like they are bubble gum wrappers in a parking lot, meandering wherever the wind blows them to.

Today matters, so use what you must make someone else's life better!

Living Like You Mean It

If you want to make the most of your life and live it with enthusiasm and zeal, reading this book is a great start! However, it will not be enough. You will need to make some tough decisions along the way. Your approach to life will need to change. As your approach changes, your attitude and the way you allocate your time will as well.

Any type of transformation requires a process of accepting change. We are constantly in "process" of becoming whatever we are meant to be.

Stay determined and disciplined, and sooner than you think, you'll find yourself living the 24/7 lifestyle and will be on the road less travelled.

A SPECIAL THANK YOU NOTE

I truly appreciate you taking the time to invest in your quality of life, your business, and your future! If you found the book to be beneficial, I would be grateful if you would leave a 5-Star review on Amazon. It would mean the world to me!

Looking for more inspiration and actionable tools to grow your business and design your perfect lifestyle? Then subscribe to the hottest new show the "Business Edge Radio" Podcast with Mitche Graf on iTunes, Stitcher, Google Play, Spotify, and others. Hear dynamic interviews with world-class Entrepreneurs as well as regular dose of meat-and-potatoes techniques that will ignite your superpower to achieve even greater things!

Additional resources can be found at www.MitcheGraf.com.

Thank you for spending this time with me, and good luck with your new set of eyes!

Mitche

Made in the USA
Monee, IL
20 May 2020

31513857R00134